To Jeff, CONGRATulations- Steve

THE LIFE
CONNECTION

HOW COACHING CHANGES LIVES

D1431961

STEVE CHANDLER

ROBERT D. REED PUBLISHERS   .   BANDON, OR

Robert D. Reed Publishers
P.O. Box 1992
Bandon, OR 97411
Phone: 541-347-9882; Fax: -9883
E-mail: 4bobreed@msn.com
Website: www.rdrpublishers.com

Front Cover Artist: Angela Hardison and Seesaw Designs
Cover: Cleone Reed
Book Designer: Debby Gwaltney

ISBN 13: 978-1-934759-54-7
ISBN 10: 1-934759-54-6

Library of Congress Control Number: 2011931509

Manufactured, Typeset, and Printed in the United States of America

FSC
www.fsc.org
MIX
Paper from
responsible sources
FSC® C011935

RAINFOREST ALLIANCE CERTIFIED

FOR KATHY

Acknowledgments

Kathryn Anne Chandler for everything.
Steve Hardison for the ultimate in coaching.
Deuce Lutui for the internal commitment.
Barbie Gummin for the life coach connection.
Maurice Bassett for the fearless club.
Michael Neill for the academy of super coaches.
Brandon Craig for sales mastery.
Rich Litvin for the confidence salon.
Todd Musselman for words and music.
Dusan Djukich for straight-line leadership.
Fred Knipe for doctoring and cabaret performing.
Sam Beckford for being the small business millionaire.
Terry Hill for the two guys quartet.
Peter and Victoria Sykes for the music school.
Regena Thomashauer for the womanly arts school.
Stephen McGhee for modeling ascendance.
Rob Owen for results now.
Ken Webb for a holly jolly Christmas.
Colin Wilson for the books.
Byron Katie for the work.
George Will for the review.

Table of Contents

*If you don't change your beliefs,
your life will be like this forever.
Is that good news?*

~ W. Somerset Maugham

DON'T YOU KNOW HOW TO LIVE?

I saw the angel in the marble,
and I carved until I set him free.

~ Michelangelo

Great coaches do work that is similar to a sculptor's work. They see what's possible in their client, and then they help the client carve the negative beliefs away. Soon the client is feeling a freedom he has never known. This freedom happened for me when I turned my life's dreams over to the hammer and chisel of my own coach, Steve Hardison.

The term "coaching" comes from the world of sports and also from the performing arts. That's why they call it coaching instead of "consulting" or "advising" or "counseling."

I remember a time when there was no coaching for people like you and me. There was only coaching for athletes and singers and actors. (Those superstars had strength coaches, voice coaches, and dialect coaches; they had quarterback coaches, golf coaches, and hitting coaches. For you and me? There were no life coaches.)

But soon a personal growth movement began as the world got more entrepreneurial and creative. Individuals became more empowered. No longer did most people work for the same huge company at the same boring job all their lives and then get a watch and retire and wear the watch in the open coffin.

Creative people and innovative small businesses were rising up. People changed jobs often, and even changed careers, and soon anyone who really wanted to succeed was considering hiring a coach.

Why not? Two heads have always been better than one. If you want something achieved, are you not better with two people on the project than one?

A lot of people have thought that this explosion of personal coaching is absurd. Why should the average person be hiring a coach? A life coach? Are you kidding me? Don't you already know about life? Don't you know how to live?

People asking those questions were missing the point. This was not about survival. This was about thriving.

Even today, people wonder if their ordinary life qualifies for "coaching." It's that whole "little old me" approach to low self-esteem and false modesty. That's the very problem that coaching ends up solving.

Mocking self-help is the ego protecting itself. However, protecting the ego keeps me isolated and shrunken down to my most survivable self. So I feel disconnected, not only from the world, but from my own potential.

*At times our own light goes out and is rekindled by
a spark from another person. Each of us has cause to
think with deep gratitude of those who have lighted
the flame within us.*

~ Dr. Albert Schweitzer

2

YOUR LIFE IS GATHERING LIGHT

*The only real purpose of a goal is to inspire you
to fall more deeply in love with life.*

~ Michael Neill

I've been conducting a coaching prosperity school for years now, so that coaches can learn to build strong practices. Because of the impact coaching has had on my own life, I am more than a true believer. I am a witness!

I have noticed that some coaches are so dedicated to helping their clients that they neglect their own practices. They don't devote themselves to getting more clients, even though it would help the world if they did.

That's one of the things coaches forget to do. They forget to become masterful at the art of enrollment and sales. But soon they notice that their life-changing work can't go on without clients. You can't change the life of a client that you do not have.

I also help coaches believe in the strength of their work. For this, I sometimes begin with the lamppost distinction. Michael Neill, the colorful author of *Supercoach*, sometimes talks about how good a coach a lamppost would be.

Many people who are just beginning as life coaches and business coaches worry about whether they have enough smarts and expertise to be an effective coach.

Consider a lamppost, Michael advises them. Let's say your client leaves his office each snowy evening and stops by a lamppost on his way home and just talks to the lamppost. Let's say he starts to do that every evening, unburdening the day's problems and vocalizing the possibilities and options for tomorrow. The lamppost will not talk back; it will just be there for him.

And by acquiring the habit of talking to his lamppost, this person finds his life is improving. It is gathering light. He feels a little less burdened each evening, and by expressing options and possibilities he even has new ideas he would not have had if he didn't talk to the lamppost.

So if a lamppost can do all this, imagine what you can do if you coach someone.

Sometimes coaching someone is as simple as listening. Then it moves to helping them get started on something they want to achieve.

3

ARE YOU ISOLATED OR CONNECTED?

*The cave you fear to enter
holds the treasure you seek.*

~ **Joseph Campbell**

To those who have asked me why I have a coach and why I've paid people to coach me through the years, I ask them why should coaching just be for athletes and actors?

They reply that athletes and actors can't *afford* to be average or mediocre. They *have* to be as good as they can be just to keep their jobs. Greatness, to them, is linked to survival. They have to be great at what they do or they're gone.

Well, so do we now. The world has gone global. No more whining about outsourcing. If someone in China can do it better than you can, game over.

To have a great life, we have to be great at what we do.

That scares a lot of people, but it excites those of us with coaches.

Why should I not want to be as good as I can be at my own career? Even if I'm not a pro athlete?

But why do you need to pay for that? Why not do it yourself?

Because coaching *works* and doing it myself never works the same way. I was *okay* by myself, but I was never *great* at anything. And even if I was, it wasn't as great as it could have been. Sometimes the things I was most proud of I later saw as unrealized potential posing as competence.

Many times people choose not to get coaching because it would be spending money on themselves! It might look selfish to their families. It might even look weak. And they've invested a lot of energy in looking a certain way. Looking like they have their act together.

But even that suggests I am an actor. That all the world's a stage and each of us play our part. Why not just go with that?

Actors have directors. Actors have coaches. Nobody questions the wisdom of that.

4
WHAT WOULD PEOPLE THINK OF ME?

Personalities don't love.
They want something.

~ Byron Katie

One of the biggest lessons I've learned from coaches is that my personality's wild attempts at pleasing others and winning their approval was working against my happiness and success.

In fact, I was *losing* the respect of others the more I tried to please them. Not to mention losing all *self*-respect.

So it was time to turn the spotlight inward—to work on myself. To take Tolstoy to heart when he said, "Everyone thinks of changing the world but no one thinks of changing himself."

Today I actually love investing money in my personal growth to change myself. I get a large return for the investment, even financially (not to mention improvements in luminosity of mind, body, and spirit).

Should I have invested that money in stocks or real estate?

I say no. I wanted to invest in me. I wanted it to go into coaching. I wanted to be fulfilled. I wanted to find out what I've got inside me.

Looking back, I see what being coached has done for me. Without it, my life would have been a long, dreary compromise. A dark festival of regrets and missed opportunities.

No one should to go their grave with their music still in them.

That's where I was headed until I met my current coach, Steve Hardison. He wasn't a therapist or a guru or a priest or a bishop or a soul mate or a boss. He was just my coach.

And from our first hour together, my life was never the same.

One quick example of what changed: Prior to working with him, since I was a little boy, I always admired writers and authors. I walked through libraries and bookstores as a child and later as a college student thinking how much I would just *love* to be an author.

But soon it was too late for that. I'd already wasted forty-eight years compromising and doing whatever I thought would keep other people happy and the wolves away from my door.

I bowed to others as well as I could.

After meeting Hardison and receiving some very energetic "life coaching" I now have written over thirty books, on topics ranging from baseball to Jane Austen to fund-raising to business success, and five of them are international bestsellers, and some others are headed there.

Does coaching really work? People ask me that.

If it didn't work, there wouldn't be coaching. It would not be growing so fast every year. As the hottest profession in the world.

And it's not just in the USA. I have been meeting lately with coaches from England and Canada and many other countries. It's not a fad; it's a force.

Why can't we all be athletes and actors and dancers and artists and singers? Get some coaching and you'll find out that we can.

5

YOUR JOURNEY TO INNER SPACE

Between stimulus and response, there is a space. In the space is the power to choose our response. In our response lies our growth and our freedom.

~ Victor Frankl

The space Victor Frankl talks about is inner space. It's not out there in the world. And even though we love stories about journeys to outer space, the journey to inner space is even more rewarding.

And that's where coaching connects.

My coach is the ultimate coach (dot net). He also coaches TV stars and pro athletes like Deuce Lutui, the best offensive lineman in the NFL. And those of you who have been following the Deuce Lutui story will want to see the latest at www. tbolitnfl.com. Please go there and read the story. Read it and send it to friends.

People today walk up to me at a seminar and say, "The story of Deuce is the story of you, and the story of you is the story of me." Well, yes! My old story was also fearful, and my new story is mine to create fresh each day. No matter how old I am. No matter what my story of age may be at the moment.

Age itself is a story.

We all have stories about what it is to be old. For example, most of us would not think of an elderly octogenarian pumping iron and getting stronger by the day.

A book called *Biomarkers* rounded up evidence that changes the story of age. It turns out that strength training in people aged eighty-four to ninety-six increases their strength fifty percent in three months and improves their health radically!

Ready to haul a box of free weights to your grandfather's house? How will that go over? It would depend on your grandfather's story of age.

Where will my own motivation come from at the age of ninety-six? My coach Steve Hardison is a young man, compared to me. Maybe he'll be there to make sure I get the most out of my life. Driving a box of weights to my house.

That's what coaches do, and that's why coaches are scorned by those who don't have coaches. This whole issue of changing beliefs and stories while *asking for help* is a sensitive one to the ego.

However, if a great athlete like Deuce Lutui can ask for help, why can't I? The great runner-philosopher George Sheehan used to say that we are all athletes, all of us. It's just that some of us are in training and some of us are not.

For me, motivation is an exciting subject. I wrote my first book about it. It was a huge subject for me because in my life I had spent so many years absolutely not motivated.

In childhood I usually took the opposite approach to being motivated. When everyone else around me seemed motivated and able to get things done... fully focused and finishing their tasks, I was the opposite. I'll never forget that on one of my report cards the teacher, in the comment section, had written, in capital letters and dashes, the word L-A-Z-Y.

I tell people that story and they get confused. "You? Lazy? You are creative, productive, and prolific! I get profound email coaching from you at four in the morning! You write two or three books a year and travel all over to speak and coach. You run your coaching prosperity school with such energy!!!"

People change.

That's the big secret that the scorners are trying to keep a secret. People change if they are open and willing.

Picture me staring at that report card and seeing the word "L-A-Z-Y" and confirming my worst fears and darkest beliefs about myself.

I concluded that I was missing something that other people had. Some kind of inner drive. I thought other people had a genetically installed sense of purpose about life that I just didn't have. Therefore I would either have to fake it in order to survive — in order to be accepted in society and civilization — or just find some way out of life, some form of suicide that didn't look too cowardly.

Well, for me, the worst thing that happened, that could have happened, did happen.

As I got into my teenage years and then off to college, I really did take a kind of way out of life (without really "knowing" that I did). I got deeply involved in alcohol addiction and rampant use of drugs; I was lucky to have come out alive. There was a time in my life when friends, family, and even medical people were saying there would be no way I would live past the age of thirty-five.

I've gone well past that number now, and I was very fortunate to be able to recover from that addiction.

People told me that when I finally joined a program for recovery that I would have to get a sponsor, and little did I know that a sponsor would be an early life coach for me.

Addiction had been an artificial form of all the things I thought I was lacking. They call alcohol "false courage" because it is. Heavy emphasis on the "false" part of the equation. When I thought I was lacking courage, I would have a few drinks and I could do things I couldn't do when I wasn't drinking. And then in college we were passing around amphetamines to get ready for our exams, and I got into that as well. It was a vicious circle. I thought I had to take speed to pass the exams that would allow me to stay in college another year so that I could drink and party and avoid the real world and see if I might not just outwit and bypass this thing called growing up and taking responsibility.

It just sounded awful to me, growing up and taking responsibility. No fun at all. Just a total *grind!* I didn't realize then that true happiness comes from growth. And growth is fun and exciting. And a person could actually participate in his own spiritual recovery and evolution.

I learned to embrace spiritual progress, not perfection. I also began to realize, thanks to my sponsor, that "responsibility" meant more power to me. It was not a shame-based concept. It did not mean I would now have more of an obligation to you.

Speed was a false form of motivation. It stole from the future to create an artificially jacked-up present moment. But then you paid back way more than you borrowed if you stayed alive; and a lot of us didn't. Many of my so-called drinking and drugging buddies are no longer alive and haven't been for a good long while.

Sometimes you borrow everything, and when they come to collect they take it all.

Later in the Army I had to stand guard late at night and so the Army doctors would give me Ritalin to stay awake. When I was in language school in the military, doctors would regularly give Ritalin because the study load was so heavy that we would study late into the night when we were studying our languages. Then we'd get drunk on weekends to unwind.

These artificial forms of motivation, courage, and purpose (or whatever that is) are destructive and damaging and actually take you (as everybody who has had any involvement in it will tell you) in the opposite direction, eventually. Because once you feel a little bit of a lift or a surge, you then pay for it five or six times over with detox, hangovers, the long crash—

and just the worst nightmarish stuff you could ever have to go through. It's just really horrific. There's no real reward to any of that.

So I was fortunate to recover from all that and go through a program of recovery that started everything all over again. It allowed me to go back over my life and eliminate the guilt, eliminate the shame, take away all the things that I had made up about myself.

That whole belief system about myself that was so negative.

Now I could start all over.

Recalculating!

A coach can help you reset your GPS.

6

YOUR MOST POWERFUL HIDDEN TOOL

*Avoid losers. If you hear someone use the words
"impossible," "never," or "too difficult" too often,
drop him or her from your social network.*

~ Nicholas Nassim Taleb

My coach Steve Hardison showed me that this little thing that everybody has called "creativity" — the ability to *create* — was really, actually, the most powerful tool we've got for building a happy, productive life.

He showed me that creativity wasn't just for finger paints in kindergarten. This thing called *creating* wasn't just about a song lyric or a new computer graphics program. You can create your *life*, and you can create your day (same thing).

It's so funny because children... when they are born and come into life... enthusiastically tap into this thing called creation. They do it so joyfully, and they love it, and they spend the whole day looking for ways to make up games and make up plays and act things out. You can turn children loose anywhere. They can play in a poor part of town among the rubbish and in an abandoned lot.

I remember when we were kids we loved any abandoned lot or a house that was under construction. We didn't need

Disneyland. We would go play anywhere and make it Disneyland because we were kids and *had not yet disconnected from our creativity.*

Grown-ups project their own lack of creativity on their young children and take them places like Disneyland or Chuck E. Cheese constantly to over-stimulate the child. They are projecting their own emptiness on the soon-to-be spoiled child. Children don't need all that. Children can (and will) create anywhere with anything.

Watch them some day. They use everything around them. They can turn anything into something fun.

How do we lose that?

We lose that by assuming personalities and then defending those personalities with our lives. No more creativity, just defense.

The creative light and spirit inside of us starts to get dim. We start to put it away. Soon we are operating... not out of creativity... but out of fear. Now I'm afraid I won't get a job. I'm afraid my spouse won't approve of me, and I'm afraid of my employer, and I'm afraid I won't raise my kids right.

And soon I'm out of energy. Because nothing takes more energy to maintain than a fear. Now I can no longer motivate myself.

People send me emails these days that say, "I don't know how to motivate myself." But if you were a child you would. You'd never even ask that question.

But now if feels like you have lost it.

You've lost the connection.

So the exciting thing for me about being a life coach is the *connection* that gets restored. That's why I call it the life coaching *connection*. When you re-connect to your core creativity, it can come back even stronger than it was in childhood.

You can re-connect, and how to do it is not a mystery.

It doesn't have to be something puzzling where you keep pleading, "I don't know how to do it... I'm all confused about it... I need help with it..." It can be something that you can access any time, any moment, and you know you can.

7

RESPONSIBILITY FOR MY ENERGY?

*Reliving past experiences through the lens of soporific
sentimentalism, is a time-honored substitute for
choosing to create the rest of your life.*

~ Will Keiper

Well, when I really got this—when I could really see
it—I took it out and field tested it and experimented with
it and found out that it really did prove to be true: That we
ourselves are responsible for our own energy levels and our
own excitement and our own enthusiasm and we can *create* it.

It doesn't come from outside of ourselves. That's the really
big awakening. That's the real big switch that gets thrown.
That's the massive turnaround that happens in a person's life,
when they finally see that the biological computer (the brain)
really works from the inside-out.

Not from the outside in.

Yet, everybody's confused about it. I get emails like,
"I want to find something that inspires me. I want to find
something that excites me. I want to find something that
calls to me."

And so they are still confused about where it comes from.
How it's generated.

Once I started to really see this inner origin, I wrote a book called **100 Ways to Motivate Yourself**, which I wrote after practicing all the techniques my coach was showing me.

I was also meeting many other people who had ways to (in adulthood) get connected again—to turn the energy switch on any time they liked. They knew how to get enthusiastic and not *find* their purpose, but *create* their purpose. Develop it. Design it. Make it up and use it for as long as it was fun and then create an even better one when the one they were using wasn't as much fun as it used to be.

This was something that became an obsession with me.

I mean, as far as I could see, everybody had this wrong!

Everybody was looking outside themselves for something that's already in there! It was like watching somebody in your household walking around saying, "Anyone seen my glasses? I can't leave the house until I find my glasses" and you see the glasses are on top of his head. And you are laughing and chuckling and they still walk around saying, "I have to find my glasses. I don't know where I put them. I know they're *out there* somewhere."

The same is true with your calling.

You think it will call from out there.

But it's on the inside.

A good coach helps you develop that calling power inside of you. Other forms of counselors or consultants help you "adjust" to life on the outside, but a coach connects you to what's inside.

IF YOU START ME UP I'LL NEVER STOP

*The secret to getting ahead
is getting started.*

~ Agatha Christie

Agatha Christie is the best-selling author of all time. Her eighty detective novels have sold over four billion copies. Yes billion, not million. So she knew something about doing great work and having an impact on the world. And, because her sales are so far ahead of everybody else's, we can say she knew something about getting ahead.

And she discovered that the secret to getting ahead was getting started.

Life coach Rich Litvin is especially good at this principle. He asks his clients to dream big. He wants to know what they are *not* doing in their lives that they always wanted to do. Then, after long conversations and deep searches into his clients' dreams he asks them to start small.

Take the smallest step imaginable toward that dream.

Picture the smallest step you can picture, and now do that step.

And now you've started.

9

HOW TO BANKRUPT A FOOL

To bankrupt a fool, give him information.

~ Nassim Nicholas Taleb

People make the mistake of stuffing their heads with words and numbers. They pile in more and more information hoping that sooner or later they'll have enough information to finally succeed at something.

But information only goes so far... and if you get too overloaded with it, you can go bankrupt learning to succeed instead of going out there and succeeding.

Some people spend their whole lives preparing to live.

Which is why the programs life coaches offer always have a lot of action in them. Transformation works better than information, and you can only transform through practice.

Author/coach Michael Neill and I recently co-presented a six-month seminar for twenty-two people from all over the world. It was called "Financially Fearless." During one of the last sessions, we passed out the above quote from Nassim Taleb on how to bankrupt a fool.

We wanted to draw a dramatic distinction between information, a gluttony of which can bankrupt you, and transformation, which will leave you leaner and stronger. Most of the people in the room were coaches by profession. They were in the business of *delivering* transformation, so they got the point faster than most people would.

I work with coaches every day. They have become my professional coaching focus. I love the work they do in people's lives. My role in coaching them is to help them build strong practices and make a good living so they can go on serving people in the profound way they do.

Because it's hard to be good at coaching people to succeed if you are not successful yourself. You don't have a lot of real world experience to draw on. It's mostly theory. You merely chat.

Most coaches are so busy helping others reach their goals and live their dreams that they neglect their own financial strength. They forget to set up a strong system for growing their practice. That's where the work I do comes in. I've done a number of coaching prosperity schools where I help coaches gain a mastery level of business prosperity. They learn to acquire clients easily.

In my school, there is no information.

Why bankrupt these coaches?

It's transformation or nothing.

10

YOU AND THE UNIVERSE ARE ONE

*Everything is dependent on everything else, everything
is connected, nothing is separate. Therefore everything
is going in the only way it can go. If people were
different everything would be different. They are what
they are, so everything is as it is.*

~ G.I. Gurdjieff

Everything is connected and nothing is separate.

But then why do we feel so disconnected?

It could be all the stories we believe about having and being separate identities that need to "succeed" on their own. Good coaching re-awakens you—in your heart and mind—to the connection to the universe that is already there. The connection you feel when you are feeling joyful and the connection that seems to go away when fear creeps in.

One good way back to our universal connection is the internet, which gives us a technological link that mirrors the connection that's already there. And for all the knocking of social networks and the games people play on their computers, this internet is a good thing. This is a good time to be alive.

We've entered a very exciting age. People—even "average people" like you and me—can take their talent directly to the whole world right now. We don't have to climb through all the layers of permission and approval we used to have to climb in the old hierarchical days.

That's why life coaching is such a hot thing and growing like crazy. Because people have more ways to succeed at life than ever before. Why not get a coach and just make it happen?

If you want to be an author, for example, you don't have to figure out a way to get some publisher or agent to approve of your work before you can get it published. You don't have to battle for shelf space in a bookstore any longer. You just hit a key on your keyboard and you can be published.

Because these layers of hierarchical approval are disappearing, anyone can form a garage band, rehearse, write some songs, put up a website and sell a downloadable album. People can write eBooks and sell them without anyone ever approving of anything. No permission necessary.

And because of this expanded opportunity for everyone, no one really has to settle for a mediocre performance of their profession. Which is exactly why coaching is flourishing.

One of my clients a few years ago had an okay day job but really wanted to be a poet. He'd written poetry and other things on the side, but he wanted to see how good he could really be. So he hired me to coach him. I'd been a writer all my life, and a full time songwriter for a number of years and even had published some poems when I was younger. So I was able to coach his writing as well as his whole life that circled around the writing. That's the beauty of life coaching: it coaches the whole life, not just the special chosen focus.

My client learned to challenge himself more and more as a writer and it wasn't long before literary magazines all over the country were eagerly accepting his poems. He was giving readings. The coaching relationship was very fulfilling for both of us.

At that same time I also had a coaching client who was president of an aluminum manufacturing company. What did those two clients have in common? What is the common denominator between aluminum pellets and poetry? It was this: they both had goals and dreams of higher achievement.

The great American philosopher Ralph Waldo Emerson said, "Our chief want in life is somebody who will make us do what we can."

Notice he said "chief" want and not "one of our many wants." It's what we want *more than anything else*. To find somebody who will make us do what we can! Is there any wonder, then, that coaching has bloomed and blossomed?

A lot of people laugh at the very idea of my having a life coach. *Why do you need a coach for your life? Don't you already know how to live?*

Apparently not! Because without my coach, I was living differently than I live right now.

I was underachieving but I didn't know why. Like most people, I had talents I was afraid of. I had courage and willpower I had no idea existed. I could go on for many pages about all the things I found in me through the coaching connection.

But is it really so mysterious? I wrote a book about what happened to me when I was coached by my coach... how it allowed me to completely reinvent myself. I talked about how little kids know where to go to get a feeling of pure joy... (by constantly trying to do things they have never done).

The famous cry of, "Look Ma, no hands!" is a cry of joy, because the child wasn't satisfied with just riding the bike. The child tries riding it with hands up in the air, and the thrill is right there. There is no more joyful cry than when you hear a child yelling, "I did it! I did it!"

It's doing things that brings a child joy. As grownups, we have forgotten that. We somehow think that it's *feeling things* that will lead to our happiness. We've lost touch with what we once knew. We've disconnected from the spirit.

Coaching was my re-connection. It worked for me.

Is it a big puzzle that if something works for improving the way you play a game like golf it might also work for the game of life?

I've known men who have hired golf coaches to improve their game and… oh my goodness… how their games improved! Sometimes quite dramatically.

They did this because golf had become important to them.

They reached a point in their progress where they felt stuck. Yet they were passionately curious about how good they could be if they could somehow take their game to another level. That's why they hired their coach.

What if they became as passionately curious about their lives? What if they made their whole lives as important their golf game? Because a person can feel stuck there, too. Right? About life itself? A person can certainly wonder what life might feel like if it were taken to a whole new level of effectiveness and self-expression. And not just some hypothetical person either.

May I suggest that it could be every person?

Well maybe not. Maybe not a person who had hardened into a lot of pride in his existing permanent identity. Not if he was afraid to let go of his well-rehearsed self. He would laugh at the idea of a coach. He would have to. To maintain who he was.

A top business owner called me and said she had read one of my books and had some questions about this life coaching stuff I wrote about.

"Why would I need that?" she asked.

"You never need it," I said. "You just want it. Or you don't want it."

"What's the point of it?"

I thought about it and finally said to her, "What if you had never painted anything but were hired to paint a mural on the front wall of a new museum in your community. Would you take some art lessons? Would you get help? Most people would. So, if that is so, maybe you can also see your life as a creative work of art."

11

WORK THAT CAUSES INSPIRATION

Just as appetite comes by eating,
so work brings inspiration,
if inspiration is not discernible at the beginning.

~ Igor Stravinsky

One of the greatest sports coaches of all time was John Wooden. He coached basketball for UCLA and won more national championships than any coach before or since. His motto was, "Make each day your masterpiece." And although Wooden was a basketball coach by profession, his former players all talk about the life lessons he taught.

Wooden was a life coach.

He coached the whole life of the player, not just one skill. His teams won all those championships because of that. Other more narrowly focused, strictly-basketball coaches lost the games they played against Wooden's teams.

I was sent an *LA Times* article on basketball coach Nancy Lieberman by a client and friend.

One of the many wonderful things about being in this work called life coaching is that people are always sending me things. Whenever they see something exciting about how a coach has innovatively changed people's lives, they send it to me. They know I love this stuff.

So I am now reading about a basketball coach named Nancy Lieberman. She talked about going into Harlem as a "little white Jewish girl with flaming red hair. I was dribbling my ball like I lived there." She went on to become a star basketball player and now, forty years later, she is the first woman to coach a team in the NBA Development league, just a step away from the NBA itself.

Lieberman took the job coaching the Texas Legends. After a Hall of Fame career as a college, Olympic, and pro star. She says, "I've never known what my limits are and I'm not afraid to find out."

Can you sense how far away that is from psychotherapy?

Lieberman knew basketball inside and out. But great sports coaches know that to really develop their players they need to do *more* than coach basketball.

They need to coach the whole person.

So Lieberman called Pittsburgh Steelers coach Mike Tomlin and said, "I'm a white, fifty-two-year-old woman about to coach a predominantly African-American team. I need to know how I can help these guys."

They met together for hours. The topic wasn't basketball. It was leadership and personal growth.

One of the all-time great UCLA basketball players was Bill Walton. He played for John Wooden and never forgot the experience. In his Foreword to Wooden's biography *They Call Me Coach* Walton writes, "Coach Wooden is a humble, private man who has selflessly devoted his life to make other people's lives better. John Wooden, while hired to coach basketball, never stopped at something so simple. He taught life at UCLA for twenty-seven years before officially retiring in 1975, establishing records for success that will never be touched."

The records came because he taught life.

12

CORPORATIONS ARE WAKING UP!

Corporations have hired me to come in and train their managers on how to coach people. They understand that coaching is different than managing. They have gotten wind of this phenomenon called coaching.

Managing is not getting the job done anymore. It's based on an outdated hierarchical system of military command. It is most often an attempt to control other people, while coaching's intention is to empower other people.

How does coaching empower other people?

There's no one way. Coaching is different with every coach. It's creative. It doesn't follow rules. So there's a kind of fierce poetry to the art of coaching. The great coaches are all different. They would have to be, because they are calling on so much unique intuition and inner creativity to coach. It's not a science.

However. It does seem to work. When you are finished with your coaching session you have more power than you had before. Whereas, when you are finished being managed you have no more power; you've just been managed.

When managers learn to coach instead of control, they bring out the best in their people. I wrote a book with Duane Black *(The Hands-Off Manager)* on how much more productive and innovative organizations are when the old management style of military-type bossing is replaced with coaching.

Which always brings up the worry (and the fear in the corporate mind) that coaching might be soft. Many people assume "life coaching" might be an overly compassionate, organic, new-agey, woo-woo fad that will soon fade from the scene.

It's not and it won't. Because coaching is proven to immediately boost productivity. So it won't go away.

And neither is it soft. (It's about as soft as Vince Lombardi was soft.)

In fact, a good coach is going to move you quickly into higher levels of responsibility and accountability. While a manager just kind of intimidates you and bosses you around and encourages resentment and sabotage.

Roger Evered and James Selman wrote an enlightening article for the American Management Association on "Coaching and the Art of Management." In it they talk about managers who know nothing about how to coach: "Managers act out core managerial beliefs, such as being in charge, controlling others, implementing owners' orders, prescribing behaviors and events, maintaining order, gaining and exercising command and control, and discarding the noncompliant."

And I love the cold phrase, "discarding the noncompliant." Sounds like a Hollywood divorce. It lets us know that in traditional management we are in a rather brutal world, the world of human control, not too may steps away from bullying.

The coaching world isn't as simple as that world is because coaching requires a partnership: two people co-creating a vision and then executing the vision by agreement.

When I train corporate leaders on the difference between expectation (as a management style) and agreement (as a leadership practice), they originally think I am asking them to become soft and weak. They fear I am participating in the feminization of the culture (as best illustrated in Adam Carolla's hilarious book, *In Fifty Years We'll All Be Chicks*).

In fact, when leaders learn the power of co-creating agreements instead of harboring expectations, they end up with a more accountable culture, not less. Managers who lead by expectation walk around complaining constantly that their expectations are not being met.

Creating agreements is a more powerful practice than that.

Coaching generates agreements and results. Managing generates expectations.

I coach you. You go into the world and produce a wonderful result. I talk to you in our next session about what you did and how you did it, and you become acknowledged and appreciated and therefore empowered to internalize *and repeat* your result in life, not only next week but also long after the coaching contract is over.

13

WHY AREN'T YOU CONNECTED?

Addressing a wide range of issues, including work, finances, health, relationships, education, spiritual development, and recreation, life coaching looks to close the gap between our dreams and the realities of our existence.

~ Dr. Nathaniel Branden

The great British novelist E.M. Forster had a very simple prescription for all artists, writers, and people in life who wanted to succeed and be effective. He said: "Only connect."

When I taught a public speaking class at a university in California I told my students that if I had but five seconds to teach the whole year's class I would say this... then I walked to the board and wrote: ONLY CONNECT.

Because public speaking, writing, coaching, and leadership — in anything (including parenting) — is all about connecting with the other person. It is *not* about being impressive and looking like I've got my act together.

We all long to be connected. We often use "falling in love" as a way to connect to the joy that created the universe. It's no accident that it's sometimes called "hooking up."

Some girl I love sent me a quote the other day by Henry David Thoreau, and it expressed something startling and beautiful to me. The quote was about a snowflake. Thoreau said,

> How full of the creative genius is the air in which these are generated! I should hardly admire more if real stars fell and lodged on my coat. Nature is full of genius, full of the divinity, so that not a snowflake escapes its fashioning hand.

Snowflakes, when you look at them closely, show you that creative genius is in the air. Just waiting for us to breathe it in and breathe it out and, by so doing, connect.

When John Lennon and Paul McCartney connected, there was nothing less than the miracle of Beatles music spreading across the universe (like strawberry fields) forever. When creative people connect, amazing things happen.

But why should such connections only happen for rock stars, film crews, and the creative teams at Apple?

You can connect, too.

Putting two people together in a creative setting can have marvelously explosive results. *Fast Company* had a recent article by Danielle Sacks on the history of advertising agencies. She wrote,

> Before 1960, ad making was a solitary practice. Copywriters toiled away to pitch a product, then handed them off to an art director who translated them into an illustration or a photograph. Creative director Bill Bernbach (the B in DDB) changed all that when he recognized that pairing wordsmith and artist could spark genius.

Life coaching is like pairing wordsmith and artist. The coach is the wordsmith and the client is the artist. Any individual life on this planet can be treated and executed like a work of art.

Consider the man who lovingly and carefully sits in his garage building a birdhouse. All the care and patience of a creative artist come into play. Why will he not build his whole life that same way? After all, he knows *how*!

But once the work on the birdhouse is finished he re-enters the world of real threatening life. It is, therefore, a world of nervous reaction. Instead of creating the relationships he wishes to have with his family and others, he *reacts* to those people and makes a scary movie out of his world.

A coach can change all that. A coach can connect with you and then connect you to the creativity that is the real true hidden you.

Most adults respond to coaching because most adults have become disconnected.

Like Picasso said, every child is born an artist, and the real trick in life is to *remain* an artist. Because most of us don't. Because most of us feel the disconnect right around junior high school.

We disconnect from our original savage grace and creativity in the name of being accepted and liked and not embarrassing ourselves with our peers. We sell out for approval. We grow up and try to get jobs and families. It's hard. We form safe and insincere personalities. We disconnect from our courage and our power.

Then a coach comes along.

14

COACHING CAN BE CHALLENGING

Some of the biggest breakthroughs with my coaching clients, and even in my own life, have come from seeing the benefits of challenge. I've seen how it benefits me to challenge myself.

Problems that challenge me benefit me.

When I can see it that way I have a completely different life. I'm not just avoiding things with my day.

Most people new to the coaching process reveal that they have an avoidance-based life. They wake up in the morning and mentally picture what they dread. Then they try to figure out how they are going to avoid what they dread. It's a life of creative aversion.

They wake up and they say, "What do I *have* to do? What are my obligations? And what do I hope does not happen?"

This is a life that is subconsciously being lived with a mission to avoid challenges. Because this person doesn't see the benefit of challenge. They see challenge as an affront and insult to the comfortable life; and so they try to avoid it and end up being *more* challenged than other people, in the long run, because of all the challenges they avoid.

Let's look at the physical side of this. Studies have shown (and I refer you to the book, *Biomarkers*, but you can check this out for yourself with your own body) that people who challenge themselves physically end up feeling better — having a better life, having more energy, having more clarity, having more spirit. Feeling stronger. Actually *being* stronger.

They did studies with people in their eighties and nineties and gently they began bringing weights in. What a horrible thing — poor old eighty-five year olds — you are going to make them lift weights? Are you kidding? Are you sick? What is this — some kind of death camp experiment? No. These people got stronger and more energetic. Their heart health got better, their outlook got better, and their lung capacity improved. Their metabolism was better, their nervous system was better, and the circulation in their bodies really got better from lifting weights — at the age of eighty — at the age of ninety.

What a graphic, measurable example of the benefit of challenge.

Even though, in our society, the very word "challenge" makes people sad. Sometimes I meet a new client and ask where she wants to begin and she hangs her head in sorrow and says, "I have challenges."

I'll have clients come to me frightened by some "problem" (and notice that I'm putting the word "problem" in quotes), and they're upset that they even have to deal with the problem. They are not seeing that dealing with this problem is going to make them happier and stronger and better as a human being. It's like lifting a weight. The arm strengthens and the weight feels progressively lighter.

How to get people to see the benefit of challenge?

First of all, the coach sees it right away. One of the wonderful aspects of coaching is that the coach sees the hidden benefit immediately.

Even if the client does not.

So what is that first step for the client? Sitting down and repeating affirmations in the morning? "Challenges benefit me... challenges benefit me." That's not bad — that could be a good start. But he would want to follow it up with experimentation and see if challenges benefit him. Accept the challenges and take them on. Dance with them until the challenges are too tired to stand any longer.

Challenging yourself gives you a relationship to challenge that's beneficial. You begin to see it as something that serves you and feeds you and gives you energy and gives you strengths. The more I challenge myself, the less the outside world throws things at me that look like obstacles and huge problems that are hard to overcome. These now look like easy challenges. I've been challenging myself all week—show me what you've got. What do you have? Throw your challenge at me because I love challenge.

If we could learn through experience to love challenge, then challenges would no longer be filed in the category in my brain called "What's wrong with life? Why can't life just be pure comfort? Why won't things and lovers come along to make me happy?"

Werner Erhard is credited with bringing coaching into everyday life. Eliezer Sobel, author of *The 99th Monkey*, said this about Erhard:

> Werner Erhard once bluntly put it to me, staring right into my eyes, "There isn't ANYTHING that is EVER going to come along that is going to make you happy. NOTHING. Getting that is the entré into the system in which the truth lies, for the truth is always and only found *now*, in the circumstances you've got." That was quite sobering news for a truth-seeker.

15

ELVIS AS A HERO AND A FOOL

There is a yearning in all of us for mentors and heroes. It starts early. But it doesn't have to end. Your coach can be a role model as well as a mentor. Someone to look up to as well as someone to learn from.

I remember as a teenager, looking up to Elvis Presley as a hero. And his early years were very heroic.

When he was young, he would go out in front of hundreds of people... thousands of people... in an audience, and he would challenge himself to express himself from the heart and not have any fear. He knew he was singing differently, he was moving differently; he was not like anybody else in the whole world. But he would just allow that expression... that huge energy, that love of the song, the sense of ownership to simply express. Let the chips fall where they may.

If you look at some of the early films of his life, you see some of the concerts and the shows on Ed Sullivan, where you can observe the expression on his face and hear that music. It's so infectious even today. Even today with all the better production values in music, you can hear the raw beauty and the energy in the music of Elvis in his early years.

This comes from living a life of constant challenge, but it's voluntary challenge. It is absolute joyful challenge. He challenged himself and he challenged the world. Hey, look at this. Listen to this. It's different than anything you've ever seen and I don't care what you think of it.

Later in his life, that was completely turned around. His life became a life of comfort, a life of ease, a life of people around him pleasing him, the Memphis mafia feeding him drugs and deep fried peanut butter and banana sandwiches, and his life went in the opposite direction. There were no more challenges. I mean, how challenging was it to make a movie like *Clambake* or *Harem-Scarem, Girls, Girls, Girls,* or *Fun in Acapulco*? It was the same movie! There was no challenge in his world; and because there was no challenge, he lost his strength; and when his strength went away, he became obese, his voice closed up, he couldn't sing like he used to, and his life became a nightmare. He was firing guns at the television set; he was crazy, he was paranoid, and he died on the bathroom floor at the age of forty-two with all those drugs in his system.

He was a man who started seeking comfort instead of seeking challenge. He was becoming the king of comfort.

Lessons for me, all of them.

One of the callers into an Elvis webinar I did asked, "What would have been different in Elvis' life if he had had a life coach?"

He would have *lived* the last half of his life—instead of avoiding it. Coaches get you to *live*.

What happens to us when we think success and money are all we ought to go for? We find that there's nothing there when we get there. There's nothing there. There is no real security in that kind of security. There is no comfort in that comfort. It becomes fresh, new paranoia.

Second home, second boat. Third wife. Private jet. More clothes. More shoes, *more* shoes! Granite countertop!!! Re-doing the house, redoing it again. What am I looking for? What am I trying to achieve? More pleasure, more nice things.

"We like nice things."

Emptiness, all around. And if my life does not come back to me, then they can bring the curtain down.

We are going out to dinner with a couple. They keep saying at dinner, "We like nice things" but they're just miserable people. OK, these things are nice, yeah, but... *you*?

That's what seeking comfort does. It leads to huge discomfort. In the soul. But what about turning that around? How about seeing the value of challenge?

I was coaching a very creative person who is a client of mine, and we were doing a session over Skype one night, and he was beaming. His life had taken off; he was serving so many people, and he was a very happy person and he looked into the camera on Skype, looked at me, and he said, "This recession is the best thing that's ever happened to this country."

I loved that. What joy in that statement! But the reason he could say that was because of how he valued challenge. How he himself had used challenge to increase his creativity and productivity.

Valuing challenge is what gets you the life that you saw when you were younger. When you were a kid and you said, "Hey, let's see if we can jump off *this*!"

Remember that? Challenge. We knew intuitively that's where the fun was. That's where the *real* fun was—in challenges—not in comfort. Making a child comfortable is the same as making him bored.

I mean what if you walked up to a really energetic child and said, "Well, I know you are playing and you're running and you're jumping off things and you're crashing your bike and you think it's fun, but it looks really dangerous so I want to give you comfort instead. Come on in the house; we're going to let you lie on the couch and give you a lot of chocolate and food and put on a DVD, sweetheart. We're going to give you some comfort."

The child wouldn't buy it. The adult would, but the child would prefer jumping off the roof of the house onto a discarded mattress.

But parents often project their own misguided "need" for comfort on their children and start comforting them in absurdly unwelcome ways.

The world is now going through a "recession," which is a polite, comfortable word for it. It is going through a challenging time because credit cards and free homes have been taken away from people—"Sorry, no more free money."

People can interpret this as tragedy. They can say it's shocking. I see clips on TV of people rioting, burning cars, and smashing windows because the retirement age in their country was going to be raised from sixty to sixty-two. "Oh no! What a horror, what a nightmare; we have to work two more years."

We don't want work or challenge! We want comfort! We want retirement. We want out.

Or so we think.

I have never heard of a person on his deathbed looking back on his life and saying, "What a great life I've had and what I most loved were the long spans of comfort I experienced. Let me recount those hours of my life where I felt so comfortable I didn't even know I was there. And that was the real greatness of life—being taken care of like an infant. I'm glad I'm here attached to all these tubes. It's like the womb almost. I have gone back to those wonderful days of yesteryear. Being fed by others, not having to do anything."

No one ever talks that way at the end of his life. People talk about the challenges they faced. People talk about what they went up against.

I remember my father talking about World War II. War is hell, but not in his memory.

And as he got older he would talk about the adventurous things he did when he grew up poor, in Parker, Arizona. The challenges the family had! How they took in laundry at night and they all worked on it. His eyes lit up. You could see it in his face. Those were the great times.

He made a lot of money in business and then retired early to drink all day and sit in front of the TV set and watch re-runs of *Happy Days*. That wasn't the part of his life that he recounted. He never wanted to talk about that phase.

Isn't that funny? He never wanted to talk about the very thing he worked so hard all his life for, an early retirement! That's what the future will do for you. That's what living in the future of comfort produces. Shame.

He never said, about his retirement, "Oh that was so satisfying. To just be able to get up and make myself a martini, take a couple of Valium, and then go take a nap. Now that made my life worth it."

That was the shameful part of his life. That was the part he didn't want to talk about.

He wanted to talk about the challenges. Because when he was truly alive, he was amazing at handling challenges.

And if we got real honest, and if we really looked at where joy comes from, we would start to welcome challenges. We would start to challenge ourselves *more*.

I wake up. Look at my calendar. Do I have space in my day to challenge myself with something? Who am I afraid to call that I am going to call today? What kind of physical accomplishment can I do that I wasn't going to do?

Challenge brings joy, but most people devote their adult lives to avoiding challenges. Because they think a challenge shouldn't be there. A challenge is a problem. It's an obstacle. It's something they need to avoid.

Coaching presents a challenge to people.

Good coaching, especially. Which is one of the reasons it's mocked by outsiders.

With my coach listening to me make excuses for why I have not taken big bold action in pursuit of my mission, there is nowhere to hide.

My friend Matt Furey coaches people in physical fitness (he was a national champion wrestler and world champion martial artist). He also coaches people on how to create successful internet businesses like he did. We were exchanging emails the other day about what it meant to be a time warrior (being violently uncompromising about where you spend your time) and he said,

> One of my friends in college wrestling had the
> best response to a friend who told him he should

be more sociable so people would like him: "I'm not here to make friends," he said. "I'm here to win a national title." He did. And people liked that about him.

I sit across from my coach. I take out my notebook. He is reading the email I sent him last night about what I wanted to work on in our coaching session. He says, "I'm going to challenge you right now; are you open to that?"

I feel my heart skip, and then I realize that this is always when the good stuff happens.

16

YOU DON'T NEED TO ATTRACT

I speak slowly. I don't get all psyched up and pumped up. I don't transfer my energy to you. I don't want to get *you* psyched up and pumped up. I don't live with passion—at least not in my audio recordings. So, let's get that straight. I do this deliberately. I speak slowly. I slow everything down.

I want you to be able to hear this at a level that you are not all pumped up and excited about, but a level that goes in there (into the subconscious part of your system—into every cell in your body) and becomes an operating principle instead of just information. Something you *know*. It might become a place to come from. I want to slow your mind down. I don't want you racing out ahead of what I am talking about into your own future.

This future-racing that we do is really the problem as far as success is concerned. If people would simply slow down and focus on the beautiful details right here.

Choose a few good moneymaking skills and practice them slowly. Wonderful things would happen.

But rather than practicing core skills, I find my client, Reed, pasting photos all over his office… photos of hot cars and hot women and seaside mansions. Michael Buble is singing loudly from the speakers on Reed's computer:

So you want to be a rock star
with blue-eyed bunnies in your bed
well remember when you're rich
that you sold yourself for this
you'll be famous cause you're dead

Reed explains to me that he is utilizing the law of attraction. He says that one cannot have blue-eyed bunnies in one's bed without first picturing them there.

I sit Reed down for his coaching session, and I say, "Let's take this idea of attraction first. If you really want to succeed, one of the first things you want to eliminate from your mind is this thing called attraction."

Reed looks stunned. His whole office is geared up for a harmonic convergence. He believes he can create a vortex for abundance in his mind and his very room.

"I'm trying to develop a passion," he says, "for attracting what I want. I'm including passion on that list."

Reed points to the word "PASSION!" written in deep purple on his wall.

He says, "I want to learn to live with passion."

I look at Reed and he looks exhausted. I can tell he's been working on his room a long time.

Reed is not unusual. Spoiled as a child, he has been conditioned to always wonder whose boots he has to lick to get what he wants. Who will give it to him? The universe? I need to tell him that there is no universe. Can he handle that yet?

Reed is not unusual.

Prospective coaching clients often begin their calls with these words, "I want to attract things into my life. I want to find a way to attract wealth. I want to find a way to attract a spouse. I want to find a way to attract customers to my website. I want to find a way to attract clients into my world."

I recommend that they drop that. I ask them to look back through their lives and notice how it does not work. I would only drop it because it does not work.

I've worked with people for over twenty years and I have never seen "attraction" work. Therefore I would drop it from my repertoire (my vocabulary), especially from inside that part of my mind that carries the morbid, toxic beliefs around with me that keep me from succeeding.

This thing called attraction—attracting a partner, attracting customers, attracting money, attracting wealth, attracting good contacts and stuff—is often associated with life coaching. Or new age spirituality wherein we harmonize with the vortex and cuddle up with the universe so that the universe finally begins to bless us.

It's childhood all over again. What do I think Mom's going to give me for my birthday?? It's exciting! What am I going to *get*? It's all about wishing and hoping for things, so it's the *opposite* of what good coaching brings about.

Coaching empowers people. Coaching does not relate to what everyone else is calling "the universe."

I want to drop "attraction" as a strategy only because it doesn't work. Have I repeated that enough times? Because repetition (annoying as it is) has you get it. So you might end up not liking me, *but* getting it. So that would be OK with me. I mean, that would be perfect for me. I'm not here to attract admirers. I'm really here to have these principles get inside people who are interested in how and why coaching works.

Once I drop my love affair with the idea of attraction, what can I replace it with? I mean, I might *want* a spouse or a partner. Am I to now be deliberately *un*attractive? I might *want* customers or clients. I might *want* wealth coming into my life. So if I'm not going to be utilizing the law of attraction, if I'm not going to sit quietly and picture these things coming into my world, then what can I do instead?

What I recommend for people to do is make a difference. To actually make a difference all day, every day, by using creation. By substituting creation for where they once had attraction as their operating system. Rather than attracting a partner, I want to create a relationship. Now I can become active. I can join clubs; I join church groups and connect with civilization.

I remember once, many years ago, I joined a group of single parents with children. I had full custody of my kids, as did the other single parents in our group, and it was really fun. But I *created* that activity, and so I made my life different than it was, which is called *making a difference.*

Making a difference has you be creative throughout the day instead of sitting back wondering how to attract things.

Here's the main problem with attraction as an operating principle. This is why it's dysfunctional. Attraction immediately assumes that there are things (people, money, whatever) outside of you, out there somewhere, that need to come into your world for you to be happy. That's what attraction is all about. Moving something from the outside to the inside. Therefore the whole theme of attraction…. the whole principle of attraction… is that *you are not enough.*

You don't have what it takes.

That's the starting point. That's the beginning premise. You are not enough. You are incomplete. You are missing something major. You are a damaged self.

And that's a very weak way to start your day.

To believe that you don't have… inside of you… the resources to make you happy. You need to have it all come to you from the outside. You need to have it come in from what you fearfully regard as "the universe." It's the same old *punishing God* paranoia that the ancients had, only dressed up in a new age "universe" language.

To be complete? I need to attract, from the universe, a beautiful new partner, more clients, more money, a perfect job, more hits on the website! With attraction as my belief, all these things must come to me from the outside for me to be happy.

That has me walking around deficient as a human. And when my self-concept is deficiency, how bold and confident can I be in my communications today? It's my communications that will bring me success, not the universe. But because I have begun my day focusing on my laundry list of deficiencies (dressed up as goals and dreams) I am weak and scared. Because I am not enough.

I am trying to "attract" what would complete me, and my whole day is about that.

It leads to low self-esteem. It leads to becoming someone that other people don't want to be around. We love being around people who have enough. Who love their lives, who are in love with life because they've got everything they would ever need to be happy. We love being around people like that and we are (dare I say it—I shouldn't even say this) we are *attracted* to people like that.

My coach taught me to turn my life around completely, so that my focus was on strengthening the *inside* instead of focusing so much on what was missing from the outside.

My coach Steve Hardison taught me that when I did look to the outside, it was always to see where I might be able to make a difference. Rather than to whom I needed to impress or win over. I was to look for where I could make a difference in someone's life.

17
HOW TO MAKE A REAL DIFFERENCE

I once worked with a person by the name of Lyndon Duke. Lyndon lived up in Oregon and was a coach and mentor of mine—and he communicated with me in many ways. He used to send me cassettes—coaching cassettes—where he talked directly to me on the cassette! I'd never heard of that. But it's part of what is crazy and effective about coaching.

There is no standard conformity for everyone to imitate. Every coach is different.

And so I would drive around listening to these cassettes over and over. He was a powerful man, a wonderful gentle philosopher and his specialty was *the linguistics of suicide.*

How interesting and strange.

It sounded negative. The linguistics of suicide! It sounded dark, but it wasn't. It was his way of bringing the light.

Because he had become so good and accomplished studying suicide notes, finding out what would have a person be that low on the scale of motivation, inspiration, spirit, that they would write a suicide note or that they would even consider that. What he discovered over the years in his research was that people in that state of mind were not making any difference. In their opinion.

They felt that their being on this planet made no difference to anyone else.

So when Lyndon worked with them, he knew that if he could get them to the point where they were making a difference—no matter how small—and they *knew* they were making a difference, their lives would take on new meaning. Their lives would actually *become meaningful.*

"If something makes no difference," he would say, "it has no meaning."

Over and over he would repeat that to me, so that I would never forget the power of difference-making. "Meaning is the difference something makes. If it makes no difference it has no meaning."

At the same time that I'd discovered Lyndon, I was also being coached by Steve Hardison. I gave Steve one of Lyndon's cassettes to listen to. I was afraid that he might be irritated that I was learning from someone other than him, but he had the opposite reaction.

"Wow!" he said when he heard Lyndon's tape. "That dude is amazing! He's powerful!"

Steve thought it was absolutely great that I was learning from him.

Lyndon convinced me that if you could get a seemingly hopeless person to start making even a tiny difference, it would change everything in their lives.

Difference making is also the key to creating wealth; it's the key to creating relationships; it's the key to creating clients, creating customers, and creating the life you want. I want to look at what differences I can make today in the lives of my clients by helping them see the differences *they* can start making.

If a person is contacting me and wanting to talk, I want to ask myself, "How can I contribute to this person's life? What could I do that would make a difference right now?" Instead of, "How am I coming across?"

I've had so many of my clients who tell me they're going to communicate with a prospective customer and "I don't want to *come across* like this_____." I want to re-connect them to the spirit that connects everything by asking, "What kind of a difference can you make in their lives today?" Instead of allowing them to continue to worry about how they are coming across.

Stop coming across. Start making a difference.

People are so incredibly obsessed throughout the day with how they are coming across! "I'm going to send this email. Look at it, Steve, okay? How do you think this email will go over? How will I come across sending an email like this?"

And that's the whole fallacy of attraction as a goal. That's the whole fallacy of trying to manipulate other people's love and approval. It never works. It never holds. In fact, it backfires. The more obsessed I am with how I am coming across, the more repulsed other people are by my phony attempts to impress them. The less they want to be with me.

You know this.

You've been to dinner parties and similar gatherings where it's obvious when a person is trying to make an impression and win approval. They are trying so hard to come across a certain way that they become repulsive and you look at your friend and you kind of smile like, "Oh, my gosh. What a jerk!" And your friend says, "Yes. He is trying a little too hard isn't he?"

And this is why *wondering how I am coming across* will never work for me. I want to replace it with different questions: What difference can I make? How can I contribute? How can I help?

Whenever I value difference-making in my world, my world literally becomes different. I am soon living a life of creating relationships, creating money, creating clients and customers, and creating what I want instead of trying to attract it.

Creating by making a difference.

Trying to attract friends and wealth from outside of me solidifies my self-concept as deficient, defective, and not enough. I want to shift that to a whole, complete, and totally happy me.

18
THE AWAKENING SLAVE

If you want to live a life and have a professional career characterized by velocity and power, then you will allow yourself to see and experience the source of that power. It's your inner stance. It's you.

~ Dusan Djukich

Susan Motheral is a mentor and consultant to women and a friend of mine. She specializes in helping women find the happiness and pleasure that is sometimes lost in the name of altruistic, saintly self-sacrifice... living for others.

We talked recently about boundaries and saying NO and the ability to eliminate clutter and complicated confusion in life. How a happy and renewed love of life most often involves taking things away, instead of continuously trying to add things. Like Michelangelo did with his art... he obtained a huge block of marble from the quarry and then proceeded to chop and carve away.

Great writers do that with their manuscripts. The editing and cutting is where the magic emerges.

Susan sent me a postcard after our talk. It was a Michelangelo stone sculpture called *The Awakening Slave*... and the beautiful statue is only partially carved from the stone block. Susan was cleaning her home office when she coincidentally came upon this card.

She writes, "Look at what I found. Isn't the title just the best for the topic of cleaning...? *The Awakening Slave.* And that delicious quotation from the artist, Michelangelo, comes to mind: 'I saw the angel in the marble and carved until I set him free.'"

Coaching, when it's great, does that too.

19

HOW TO NOT EVER GROW UP

One's relationship to a life coach is often a long-term project, because there need be no end to the process of learning and growth. This is why many champion athletes and high performing business executives retain coaches long after the time they have become successful.

~ Dr. Nathaniel Branden

One of the ways I coach people is via email. I'll often put other people's quotes in my emails that have helped people wake up to the real power inside themselves. They prefer this power to being hypnotized by the imaginary power of others. This is such a quote from Dr. Brad Blanton:

> **Wishing** *is a way to remove oneself from what is going on now.* **Hope** *is how most of us avoid growing up.*

One of my email clients didn't like that quote, and we went back and forth debating the relative value of hope. We finally agreed to the difference between hope that led to action and hope that did not. It was a great debate, provoked by Blanton's rather harsh quote.

And I enjoyed the exchange, because I am all about provocation. I enjoy provoking people so that they wake up, stand up, and start speaking for themselves, and even opposing my ideas. It's all good energy, right? Otherwise we just lie there.

And I like being wrong. One can always learn something when one is wrong. When you're right, you learn nothing... you just start to inflate. It's not good to be an inflated person. It's not strong.

Coaching is not about delivering expert advice and downloading superior wisdom. It's about provocation. There isn't much value in advice, unless you count advice like this: "Keep away from runaround Sue."

But there is great value in provocation.

20
COACHING IS ALL ABOUT PRACTICE

Coaching is such a powerful concept, especially when both coach and client commit to creating transformation and success. Two minds are better than one.

Yet, most people try to go it alone. (Thinking they look more adult and independent that way.)

I believe one of the telltale signs of a person's commitment to success is a willingness to ask for help. I know it's true in addiction recovery. Reaching out and asking for help means you are finally ready to recover. Surrender is strength.

In most of adult life we associate it with weakness. "Why do I need help? Why do I need a coach?"

No one really, ultimately, "needs" a coach. But people who are in a good hurry—people who don't want to postpone their career success any longer— *want* a coach. It's really a want—not a need.

Coaching is not therapy. When someone thinks they "need" a coach, they probably actually need therapy. Coaching is not designed to heal psychological wounds (although it can, in indirect ways). Coaching is for success. It is proactive and project-oriented. It brings out the best in people.

I love the prosperity school for coaches I conduct because it gives coaches a way to build strong practices.

It takes practice to build a practice. Coaches can learn, with practice, to become prosperous in their professions. And that actually helps their clients—who would you want coaching *you*? Someone who has a strong, proud, prosperous coaching practice, or some needy person who is struggling to pay bills?

As the 2009 baseball season progressed I watched players more closely than I usually do because of the book I was writing that year about baseball (*Two Guys Read the Box Scores*). I also read more about this thing called talent.

Because I've always had my suspicions about talent. I've even written about athletes and musicians who people assumed were "talented" but who actually practiced more than their counterparts.

I've also experienced myself being called "talented" in areas that I knew for a fact were just the result of committed practice that my coach helped me be continuously accountable for (and enthusiastic about). Yet, on the outside it looked like talent.

Leading me to laugh inside about how good coaching can make you look talented.

Now the research is pouring out to verify what I suspected all along. Talent is overrated. In fact I just finished reading a wonderful book called *Talent Is Overrated* by Geoff Colvin.

I thought that was the most impressive book I'd ever read on the subject until this week when a mentor of mine urged me to read *The Talent Code* by Daniel Coyle. Wow. That book blew me away.

Why don't we teach our children this stuff? It's so amazing how "talented" the average person can become if he or she wants to.

The Talent Code reveals the kinds of dedicated, deep practice that leads to excellence and mastery. It is so inspiring to know how much potential we *all* have in us.

Yet when we see a Tiger Woods or a Pablo Picasso or a Meryl Streep, we shake our heads and admire their "natural, inborn gifts" not realizing that we also have gifts. We just don't practice them.

Coaching comes from the world of sports. Coaching and practice go together.

21

MY INAPPROPRIATE LIMITATIONS

My two-hour coaching session was today with Steve Hardison. I enjoy being coached because I always move beyond my comfort zone. I go farther than I would have gone on my own because it's easy to fool myself about my limitations, but it's hard to fool both him and me.

That takes some twisted skill. It's not that I don't often try.

Somewhere in his home Hardison has a framed quotation from Nathaniel Branden that pretty much sums up how he approaches coaching and life:

> *I am convinced that one of the most helpful things we can do for people is to refuse to buy into their inappropriately restricted views of their limitations.*

> **~ Nathaniel Branden**

22

PLEASE DO WHAT YOU LOVE

Stephen McGhee flew into Phoenix to meet with me for four hours on the subject of conducting a coaching school. He brought his own client Mark Musselman with him. We had a small conference room at the Airport Hilton and went deep into the content of the coaching prosperity schools I've taught, one of which Stephen McGhee attended.

McGhee is one of the most dedicated and gifted coaches I have ever known. His book, *Learning to Believe the Unbelievable* can be found on Amazon and is highly recommended. After the three of us met, he went home and wrote this in his blog:

> Recently, I was in a meeting with Steve Chandler, a well-known author and leadership coach. He said, "The faster a person gets in touch with reality, the faster he will succeed" – (www.imindshift.com). These words were energized with Spirit. It was a statement that clearly sang out with truth and wisdom.
>
> One of my coaching clients has been holding onto a job he has essentially disliked for years. Sure it provided income. He was comfortable. And each night he went home feeling empty inside. Is

this how you want to live life? I can tell you, I have done this many times in life. It is not fun. Once he made the decision to move his energy into a career he loves his life has transformed. He has dropped over twenty pounds in two months. His relationship with his wife is more intimate and loving. He looks different. He walks different. He is inspiring other people in his life as an example of leadership. Getting real in one major area has transformed every arena of his life.

I invite you into the miracle of reality. My former coach and mentor Steve Hardison says "Why would you ever do anything in your life that you don't love doing?" At the time that concept struck me as incredibly insightful. Why would I do that to myself? I thought I was being responsible by being tough. Then, I began to wonder—responsible to whom? To those around me that just want me to be happy? I no longer see it that way. It was my silly idea, not my family's.

Someone on a recent flight to DC asked me about my job? I said I don't have a job. I have not had a job for twelve years and yet I do something that enlivens me every day of every week. It's lucrative and enjoyable. Some of us feel those two elements are mutually exclusive. That's not true. The story some people have is that work should be hard. You show me someone that is in touch with reality and I will show you a person that succeeds. I will show you inspiration in action. There will be poetry in that person's motion, because there is no gap in reality. It is clean and crisp.

One of the reasons people don't hire a coach and get good coaching is because they would rather look outside themselves (to circumstances) for help than inside. A coach will have them look inside. But most people prefer outside help, sometimes in the form of loans or "investments."

As if money were the answer to their lack of success.

They are the classic incompetents made *more* incompetent with a handout, not less. Give a man a fish and he eats for a day. Teach a man to fish (a good coaching session is really a fishing lesson) and he eats for a lifetime.

I just remembered a few variations on the "teach a man to fish" concept that I've always liked:

> *Give a man a fish; you have fed him for today. Teach a man to fish; and you will not have to listen to his incessant whining about how hungry he is.*

***

> *Give a man a fish; you have fed him for today. Teach a man to use the Net and he won't bother you for weeks.*

***

> *Give a man a fish; you have fed him for today. Teach a man to fish; and you have fed him for a lifetime. Teach a man to sell fish and he eats steak.*

23

CREATING A CRIME OF GENIUS

If a person suffers from acute anxiety, severe depression, or low self-esteem, he or she needs psychotherapy, not life coaching. However, if a person is basically healthy but is seeking greater fulfillment in one or another aspect of life, life coaching can be invaluable.

~ Dr. Nathaniel Branden

Today I attended a seminar on law enforcement put on by a friend and advisor who is also a detective who heads up the criminal investigations unit of the Gilbert Police Department and runs a national program that trains cops on how to catch killers.

His techniques of cutting-edge cell-phone tower tracking and other high-tech secrets of pursuit were fascinating to learn. I took many pages of notes for a book I am writing called *A Crime of Genius.* That book is the second in a series of mysteries that begins with *The Woman Who Attracted Money.*

As I sat in the seminar among all those law enforcement people with weapons on their hips taking notes, I really felt their dedication. These people put their lives on the line every day to keep the rest of us safe. We take them for granted. But they work so hard. You should have seen them taking notes and asking questions. That killer who might be on the loose is now at a real disadvantage up against these brave, smart people.

And that's the kind of thing that's fun for me to write about.

My other big motive in writing my first mystery was to introduce people to coaching. In the book my life coach Robert Chance has some coaching sessions with Madison Kerr. The reader gets to see how a coach thinks and works, and how a client's world opens like a butterfly.

In a wild kind of way I wanted to get the idea of coaching to a wider audience. I always wanted to write mysteries, so I made my hero a coach who used to be a cop. And a lot of friends and readers have told me that they never knew anything about coaching or what coaching could do until they were lured into this murder mystery.

I love writing fiction. It's just huge fun, and very, very difficult work. And I enjoy difficult work.

I didn't enjoy work before. Not before I got a coach. Before I got a coach, work was something I hated. He transformed it into something I absolutely love.

In my past life as a total victim (and I really was one!) I avoided work.

Then, through my coaching sessions, I got it. Work, when really engaged, is the most fun anyone could ever have. When it is done in a thoroughly disciplined way, it is a total joy.

Coaching has given me a life-changing message: *Only the disciplined are free.*

24

BUT THAT WOULD BE IMPOSSIBLE

I ran a writer's workshop that hosted more than twenty-five writers gathering to explore the depths of creativity, discipline and book publishing.

The workshop opened with this quote:

"Every noble work is, at first, impossible."

~ Thomas Carlyle

But what do we mean by impossible? One of the exercises I often have my coaching clients do is to sit down and create an impossible future.

Is this practical? Does it not just get their hopes up and indulge their fantasies?

Not quite.

Because we have misused the concept called "impossible." We automatically put way too many things into that category. And because we do that, we condemn ourselves to Groundhog Day. We live repetitive default days, always thinking the same thoughts and indulging the same fears. We do this day in, day out, only getting about three percent to nine percent better at what we do each year because we are not trying anything new or daringly experimental. There is no stretch. We are not thinking in new ways.

Why aren't we?

Those great ideas we get are impossible. Or so we think. And so we say.

Therefore a really effective jump-start to quantum growth in performance and achievement is to list all the "impossible" things you would like to do. And the only rule to the exercise is that they have to be, in your own mind, currently, impossible.

This is a great coaching exercise because in the past my mind would not even go there. Once I say to myself that something is impossible, I produce a total blackout. It's a shutdown category where the mind can never travel.

"I'd like to…. oh, but that's impossible."

In this coaching exercise we don't care that it's impossible because that's the rule of the game… it HAS TO BE impossible.

Strange things then happen. The impossible concept, once two people get really creative with it, and brainstorm it and work on it and look at it from every imaginable angle… no … longer…. looks… impossible.

25

NO ONE CAN BRING YOU DOWN

One day I gave a talk at a women's group of realtors. I talked about how I coach my clients… how I ask them whether they want to cede and concede and surrender all power to external circumstances like the economy, the housing market, and the temperature of the sun.

Or, if instead, they were willing to turn inward and strengthen themselves from within so that they entered the market with courage, creativity, enthusiasm, and totally inventive spunk.

I love giving these talks and the great exchanges with the audience members who ask the best questions in the world.

Here was one question: "How do I handle it when I am optimistic and opportunistic but people around me, especially family, are cynics and pessimists?"

I have no solution for that situation because there is no problem. The only "problem" is a perceived problem in the bio-computer of the person perceiving the problem. If your biological computer has been tuned recently, it can't see a problem in pessimistic family members for the same reason that it can't see a problem with autumn leaves.

I grew up in Michigan, and in the autumn the leaves on the trees would change color and then fall by my window. The autumn leaves of red and gold. Was there a problem with that? No. It's what trees do.

Same thing with people. They get emotional. They get cynical and pessimistic. Is there a problem with that? Not unless my own bio-computer is out of order.

"But there IS a problem!" said the woman realtor, "because they bring me down! They make me feel awful by the time I leave their house!"

But this is once again a misunderstanding. A faulty use of the bio-computer. Like trying to type on your keyboard when it's upside down.

Because no one can bring you down.

The brain wasn't set up to work that way. (Thank goodness. Otherwise I'd be down all the time! I'd just turn on the evening news and I'd be down in two minutes! Not because of reality, which is just fine, but because of how it's being sold to us.)

The brain was set up to only produce an emotion in response to an internal thought. Never to anything external. Not even relatives.

26

IS YOUR LIFE NOT WORKING?

Either you will make your life work,
or your life will not work.

~ Nathaniel Branden

I get contacted by a lot of people whose lives are not working. Their businesses are not working. They want coaching.

They want their lives to work again.

But they don't see the problem.

When I ask them to describe what they think is wrong, all I hear about is other people. Other people disappoint them. Or scare them. Then I hear about circumstance. The competition. The economy. Their location.

I know right away why their lives are not working. A life of expectation is a life of disappointment. A life of trying to win the approval of others is a life of fear.

My job as a coach is to restore the creative life. Because a creative life is a life of action and huge energy for achieving large and small goals; it's a life of happy flow. It's never your life that's not working. It's always just you. But that's the best news there could ever be.

27

THE COURAGE TO CHANGE

The first really powerful coaching in my life came from my sponsor. I was in a recovery program for alcohol in the 1980s and when you get serious about taking a spiritual path to recovery you get a sponsor.

I met with my sponsor at least once a week, and he coached me compassionately but in a very uncompromising way. I was held accountable for my recovery steps.

Recently I went to a twelve-step meeting with a dear friend who was celebrating her first ninety days of sobriety. Even though I have almost thirty years now of recovery from this horrific and demeaning addiction, I always learn something fortifying and illuminating at these meetings.

Why do I include this meeting in a book about coaching? Because none of my books would have been written had I not experienced this program of change.

Everything comes from having become clear.

There are forms of coaching everywhere. Why not make it conscious and deliberate?

At the beginning of the twelve-step meeting one recovering person read these words, words she called "the promises":

> If we are painstaking about this phase of our development, we will be amazed before we are

halfway through. We are going to know a new freedom and a new happiness. We will not regret the past nor wish to shut the door on it. We will comprehend the word serenity and we will know peace. No matter how far down the scale we have gone, we will see how our experience can benefit others. That feeling of uselessness and self-pity will disappear. We will lose interest in selfish things and gain interest in our fellows. Self-seeking will slip away. Our whole attitude and outlook upon life will change. Fear of people and of economic insecurity will leave us. We will intuitively know how to handle situations that used to baffle us. We will suddenly realize that God is doing for us what we could not do for ourselves. Are these extravagant promises? We think not. They are being fulfilled among us— sometimes quickly, sometimes slowly. They will always materialize if we work for them.

Those promises have been kept in my life.

Yet I still run into people who say that people never change.

But they are so wrong. People never change? Look at all the Before and After pictures I see every day. Look at the person who once was a daily drunk and now has a good job, a family, and is contributing to society. How big a change do you want?

My coach coached a guy who was in so much debt his life looked hopeless and his business looked doomed. After a year and a half with my coach he was debt-free and one of the wealthiest people in town. And that's just money. I only use breakthroughs in money as examples because they are so easy to measure. The real coaching breakthroughs occur in even better ways than that.

28

HELP MEANS YOU ARE A PRO

We are, each of us, angels with only one wing;
and we can only fly embracing each other.

~ Luciano de Crescenzo

Steven Pressfield has written a true masterpiece on the subject of creativity (a subject that concerns us all whether we realize it or not) called *The War of Art*.

He has a short chapter in the book called A PROFESSIONAL DOES NOT HESITATE TO ASK FOR HELP. He writes,

> Tiger Woods is the consummate professional. It would never occur to him, as it would to an amateur, that he knows everything, or can figure out everything on his own. On the contrary, he seeks out the most knowledgeable teacher and listens with both ears. The student of the game knows that the levels of revelation that can unfold in golf, as in any art, are inexhaustible.

When I was younger I would experiment by reading Emerson and allowing his philosophy and poetry to influence my mind. After I got out of recovery for alcohol I realized that living without a philosophy was not serving me.

Without my own philosophy of life to guide me I was simply attaching to the next person or thing that caught my fancy. I ran out of money and luck living this way.

Then I began experimenting with religion, psychotherapy and hypnosis. They all helped, in their own way. Now I was getting somewhere, because I was gathering a storm of momentum. Philosophical momentum.

I experimented, then, with a coach. For the first time! I hired Tom Rompel in Tucson to coach me and my business (I owned an advertising agency and PR firm). Rompel had been a student and business associate of Werner Erhard.

Was I sure I wanted to experiment with that? Wasn't Erhard made fun of by TV and movies for leading that extreme EST program?

Well, yes. But as I've later come to understand, television media is not devoted to accuracy. It's devoted to its own politically self-righteous superstitions and selling us the dark link between greed and fear. Accuracy is WAY down the list of their philosophical guidelines. So they were wrong about Werner Erhard, but they didn't mind in the least.

Tom Rompel, who would be my first coach, would be right about Werner Erhard. He had worked at his side. He knew him well. He learned so much from him. I benefitted immediately.

Erhard was dedicated to raising the consciousness of the community and increasing the effectiveness of the individual. He was moved by this purpose, just as Gandhi was moved by his purpose. Both were about strengthening the mind. Gandhi once said,

> I over-eat, I have indigestion, I go to a doctor, he gives me medicine, I am cured, I over-eat again and take his pills again. Had I not taken the pills in the first instance, I would have suffered the

punishment deserved by me, and I would not have over-eaten again. The doctor intervened and helped me to indulge myself. My body certainly felt more at ease, but my mind became weakened.

Gandhi was describing a societal magnetism toward comfort at the expense of personal, mental strength. He himself countered it with all kinds of austerities and fasting.

I was to begin my own counter of society's pull by using a coach. A coach, Tom Rompel, who later said he "had to use a two-by-four" in our sessions to get my attention.

But he got my attention.

And I learned what it was like to live on purpose.

There is a famous quote by George Bernard Shaw on the subject, and although I have read it hundreds of times (and, perhaps, so have you) it is worth repeating. When you read this quote, compare it to being lost. Because the longer I live the more I realize that life is a choice between this quote by Shaw... and being lost.

> This is the true joy in life, the being used for a purpose recognized by yourself as a mighty one; the being a force of nature instead of a feverish, selfish little clod of ailments and grievances complaining that the world will not devote itself to making you happy.
>
> I am of the opinion that my life belongs to the whole community, and as long as I live it is my privilege to do for it whatever I can.
>
> I want to be thoroughly used up when I die, for the harder I work the more I live. I rejoice in life for its own sake. Life is no 'brief candle' for me. It is a sort of splendid torch which I have got hold of for the moment, and I want to make it burn as brightly as possible before handing it on to future generations.

One of the first things Rompel did was take me into an office to show me a video of an event facilitated by his parent coaching company, Transformational Technologies.

It was called the "Manager as Coach" and was a business seminar that was shown on satellite in 1987 on TV to over ten thousand people across the U.S. They say it was the largest teleseminar ever done up to that time.

The participants were John Wooden, George Allen (Redskins coach), Red Auerbach (Celtics coach), Tim Galway (Tennis coach and the author of *The Inner Game of Tennis*), and Werner Erhard (founder of Transformational Technologies and, later, Landmark Education).

That was the first time I'd ever thought of *coaching* as something that could apply to someone outside of athletics.

29
FIND AND USE YOUR STRENGTH

Dr. Martin Seligman is someone whose work on the psychology of optimism I've praised and used and admired for years. His deep, respected research has uncovered a simple key to happiness: Use your strengths often.

But many times we forget our strengths or don't even see what they are.

I was coaching a very bright fellow who had been an accountant all his life and was just now getting into business consulting and coaching. He would attend my coaching schools and introduce himself to the other coaches as a "recovering accountant." He wanted to leave that boring life behind and enter the exciting, multi-faceted world of coaching!

But when he ventured forth to get clients he wasn't having much luck. He was not using his strength, because to him it was a weakness. So he wasn't very happy.

One of his strengths was that he was an accountant, good with numbers. He could look at a balance sheet, a business prospectus or a P&L sheet and understand it immediately. He was exactly what many business owners needed. Someone who was not afraid to look at, work with, and strengthen the numbers.

Once he saw that strength, he began to use it everywhere. He started a mastermind group that focused on Measurable

Results. It was a powerful appeal. I attended one of his mastermind sessions, which he ran with quiet strength and precision. The people in the group benefited greatly from his work. He was using his strength.

This is one of many examples of a coach seeing a client's so-called weakness for what it really so often is: the hidden strength. The client himself can't see it. But the coach can.

30

WHAT IS A COACHING CONNECTION?

A coach begins by connecting you to your own purpose. That, more than anything else, is the life coaching connection.

When I coach people, my first assignment is to connect my clients to their hidden momentum. My job is also to *disconnect* my clients from their damaged "personalities." At least, temporarily.

My own life coach reconnects me to my purpose in each session — even when my purpose shifts and changes. He doesn't care. Once we choose it we connect to it.

Otherwise my time spent between coaching sessions is wasted away dealing with the politics of human emotions. Soon I lose all energy for a joyful life.

Does coaching really work? I can't even describe it.

But let me try.

What do people want? People I talk to are always looking for more energy. They have this long list of things they think they need to get done and they say, "Boy, I wish I had more energy. What can I do for more energy? What foods can I eat that give energy? What exercise can I do?" And they look in all these different places for energy because they have so much to do.

Now one of the things that's beautiful about the concept of purpose is that *purpose actually produces energy.*

When I was a little boy I used to go swimming with friends, and I remember a couple of times while playing around in the pool, one of my friends would hold me under water. Just kind of playing around, he would hold me down there under water for a while just to scare me, just to have some fun and to make my heart race.

I never had so much energy as when that happened!

I mean, I wasn't distracted by anything. My mind didn't wander. I didn't wrestle with my options. I didn't worry about whether I would make the right decision. I had one purpose: to fight to get up above water and breathe once again.

Therefore, my energy was focused and my strength powerful and the innovation of my body movements almost magical as I threw my oppressor off and gained fresh air.

What an illustration of the power of single-minded, uninterrupted purpose! It is energy itself!

I've read a lot of accounts and I've seen some documentaries and true story movies made about people who break out of prison—even if it's an "impossible" prison to break out of. Even though the prisoners have heard about the impossibility, they plan their escape day and night.

Amazing things happen when people wake up with their purpose—a singular purpose. Throughout the day that purpose is with them and so they see things *from that purpose*. They're able to ask, of every circumstance, good or bad, "How could I use this? What's useful here based on what I'm up to?"

We can do that, too; we just forget it. In the face of all the other purposes calling to us from all the people we need to please, we forget about the power of purpose, so we don't have any. We just try to survive. We call our survival mechanism a personality and soon that personality (a collection of worries, hopes and resentments) drives our lives... the choices we make for action or non-action.

But we can, just as easily, have purpose driving our lives.

When you have purpose driving your life, you now have a way of converting "bad news" into useful news. (I'm putting bad news in quotes here because we don't really know if it's bad until years later when we can see that it was not.)

Purposeless people (personalities) who get "bad news" allow themselves to slide down the ladder and be in a bad mood. Now they're disheartened and discouraged. They're not feeling so great. That's what bad news does to them!

But, if you are *up to something*, and you are in the middle of creating actions toward a project, and some news comes in, you are able to ask, "Given what I am up to in life, how can I *use* this?" That very question is a beautiful use of this thing called purpose. I can't tell you how many times my coach has asked me that very question. "Given what you are up to, how can you use this situation?"

Often I am a prisoner and my coach just sets me free. With that one question. Like the prisoners in the movie.

When those prisoners wake up in the morning and they look around, everything they see and everyone they talk to gets filtered in through "How do I break out of this place?" and "How does that help me with the plan I've got going on to break out?" Because that's all they're thinking about—breaking free.

Being *up to something* in life gives us energy and makes us enjoy life. It is no coincidence or accident that a life coach will ask a prospective client that very question in their first conversation: "So, what are you up to these days?"

I want the clients I coach to really know the difference between how it feels to be living from purpose versus living from personality.

Personality can only be wounded and disrespected in its everlasting fight to win appreciation from others. That's what living from personality does, but living from purpose makes what other people say become unimportant. Unless I can *use it* to fulfill my purpose.

When you are up to something, energy flows into you. But when you are focused on who you think you are (your personality) energy flows *away* from you.

Maintaining a consistent affect (personality) leaves you weakened and everything else looks powerful in the face of your struggle to maintain yourself. Other people look like they have all the money and all the power, institutions look overwhelmingly powerful, health problems look like they could take you down — everything looks frightening when I'm living from my personality.

One of the most disempowering elements of one's personality is age... how *old* you are.

When I don't care about who I am and I'm in action creating and serving, my age means nothing. Some people become more and more successful, creative, and accomplished as their life moves forward — no matter what age they are. People like Clint Eastwood or Frank Lloyd Wright, who really started to blossom in their seventies and eighties because they've been on a curve of purpose that keeps eliminating what's not important.

The great ballet director George Balanchine said, "I've got more energy now than when I was younger because I know exactly what I want to do." He has *more* energy now! Now that he is older! Why? Because he knows exactly what he wants to do.

When he was younger he was probably like so many of us. He probably had so many things he was half-trying to do... or just thinking he should do.... and trying to decide what to do that the energy was robbed by all the indecision. A life full of distractions and being scattered. That's why I love the old saying, "Winners focus; losers spray."

This is a power inside of life coaching that a lot of people don't think about. It's a simple question your coach will ask you. "What do you want to create?" Or, "What is the result you would like me to help you produce?" The coaching becomes a compass.

It was amazing to watch the career of Larry Bird because he didn't have anything that you would call athleticism or any kind of natural gifts that we say other basketball players have. He was rather slow. He wasn't overly strong. There was just nothing about him that would have you say, "He would be a *great* basketball player!"

But he had a purpose.

So he was willing to do various unusual and extreme forms of practice. His purpose was so simple and so friendly to him and he would wake up with it.

So when he found that other people could guard him because he was right handed, he would practice dribbling with his left hand. So now people guarding Larry Bird didn't know which way he was going to go. It was almost as if he made himself ambidextrous! And why did he do that? He had a purpose he woke up with.

Watching a pro football game on TV I noticed that one of the players was screaming at his coach. I mean he was just losing it. He was yelling at his coach and the coach was telling him to "knock it off," and the player was yelling back at the offensive co-coordinator, and throwing a tantrum.

A tantrum is a result of over-focusing on one's personality.

> *I'm being disrespected, you hurt my feelings when you don't put me in and let me run a play and you put someone else in. I'm being disrespected. How do I look on national television when I sit out two plays that are important to the team? How am I coming across? How am I looking? I am being disrespected. Stop "dissing" me!*

That's an over-focus on personality and one's contracted identity system. That's living from personality instead of purpose.

There was another player on the same team who for almost the whole season wasn't put in the games. But he *used* that situation for his higher purpose. "I will rest, I will save my strength, I will learn, I will train, I will work out, I will be so ready when they finally do put me in that my purpose will be fulfilled and that is to make a real difference on the field."

They did put him in during the playoffs, when another player was injured, and he was so fresh and strong and *prepared for his moment* that he made all the highlight reels on ESPN after the game.

31

COACHES WANT YOUR WORD

You can't change anything by fighting or resisting it. You change something by making it obsolete through superior methods.

~ Buckminster Fuller

Making the bad thing go away is a double negative: *bad thing* and *go away* are both negative. And to change my life I want positive energy.

What the genius Buckminster Fuller is saying is an important part of why coaching works. My coach does not have me fight off bad habits. My coach has me execute superior methods of living that make the bad things a mere memory.

Often I do this with my own coaching clients. I listen as they talk to me about their problems, and I listen carefully for language that is permanent and pervasive. Whenever I find permanent and pervasive phrases in my client's talk, I stop the conversation and explore.

My client, Odessa (and that is not her real name) would always talk about herself in permanent, pervasive ways. Such as, "I always...." "I never...." Or "I have a tendency to...." Notice that these phrases describe permanent, ongoing patterns. They hint at perpetual motion machinery in the woman that drives her behavior. She obviously believes in personal patterns that explain her actions. She even tells me often, "I have a pattern of always...."

I want to break her of this mental mistake. So I tell her a story. I ask her to follow the story and see if it makes any sense to her.

One night it snowed heavily as my wife and I were watching late night TV. My wife asked me if I would shovel the walk in the morning, and I said I would do that.

The next day when she came home from work at lunchtime to have a sandwich with me, she noticed that the walk was not shoveled. She almost slipped and fell on the packed snow and ice on the walk leading up to our door.

"I thought you said you would shovel the walk," she said when she got inside.

"I have a tendency not to shovel walks," I said.

"But you said you'd do it, and if I had known you weren't serious I would have shoveled it myself this morning," she said.

"My pattern has been not to shovel," I said. "Looking back on my life, I tend not to shovel walks. It's a bad habit, I know, but it kind of runs my life and leaves me in situations like this a lot."

"I don't care about patterns or habits or tendencies," she says. "I just wanted the walk shoveled. You said you would do it."

Was my wife being unreasonable to dismiss and discount my patterns and tendencies?

Odessa said that I, myself, was being ridiculous to even float them as excuses for not doing the walk.

But that's what you are doing, Odessa, I told her. You are not doing things and then going back into your past to find the patterns and tendencies that explain it. You refuse to see that the past is over. It counts for nothing. Your word counts for everything. Your word you give *yourself* on whether you are going to do something.

32

JUICY AND SOMETIMES A LITTLE MESSY

I've been trying to stress, as a positive, exciting thing, that the best life coaches are the ones least likely to conform to anything.

They are the least likely to have practices that resemble Gabriel Byrne's laid-back psychologist on the "In Treatment" TV show.

Let's take, for example, Dr. Alison Arnold, whose website is called "Scream and Run Naked."

Can you see the provocative difference? Alison also has a book out by the same title. Her clients refer to life coach Ali as an "Awakener," "Fear liberator," and "Sparkplug." She's also an athletic coach who works with the United States Olympic gymnastics team. She's also a reality TV star who coached Scott Baio in front of the cameras for a long, hard season.

She's known as "Doc Ali" to her clients, and a rather resistant Baio, who feared her direct, confrontational tough-love coaching started calling her "Dark Alley" on the show. She was a place he didn't want to go. Transformation often looks frightening before you go there.

Ali's success is extraordinary, and like all the best coaches I know, she also enjoys *being* coached. She's been coached by the best and recalled,

> Just sitting in the room with Steve Hardison
> changed my perception of myself and the world.

My head spun as I argued with my own limitations while sitting before me was a man who completely mirrored my amazing greatness and beauty. And the way he did it blew me away. My whole being was being flooded with his intensity, and passion, about all I am, have always been, and ways I could give my gift to the world. I have been changed with every meeting I have had with Steve. Not only by the insights about my life, but more importantly through the inspiration of the way he lives his. He lives it fearlessly, lovingly, and without apology. What a model!

Ali brings up something very important here—that factor called modeling. The best life coaches work on themselves as aggressively as they work on their clients. They want to model how it's done. Unlike a consultant or therapist who only talks, a great coach will be willing to *live it for you*.

Dr. Alison Arnold is very open about sharing what she has lived and remembers thinking at one time:

I am going to Nepal to learn how to die. That cheerful thought abruptly popped me out of my morning meditation. Lovely. I was already a little nervous about this trip. Never one to give up, I took several deep, calming breaths, closed my eyes again, and immediately became aware of another question moving among the rising and falling thoughts of my chattering mind: "Have I learned yet how to live?"

Ali asked me to introduce her at a bookstore event she was speaking at when *Scream and Run Naked* first came out. I was glad to do it. Her book is one I highly recommend. In it she writes,

As we flounder along in our never-ending pursuit of happiness, we are sometimes seized by what the poet David Whyte calls "unnamed longings." We have a feeling in our gut that there is something more to life that we are missing. We long for fire and passion to fill our lives. We ache to grasp and fulfill our heart's desires. We crave a destiny of our own. In short, we want to be alive.

From coaching athletes to average people who just want to *live* more than they are living, Ali sees it all as the same evolutionary leap. "Do you ever feel like you are 'asleep at the wheel' of your own life?" she asks. "What do you feel you are missing in your life and how are you going to find it? Do you want to die before learning what it means to be truly alive? To feel passion and wonder and excitement once again?"

Feeling her own life had been "flat-lined" and with more questions than answers, Alison traveled to Nepal and Thailand to learn from Buddhist monks. Buddhism, particularly as it is practiced in the West, is more of a non-sectarian philosophy than a religion. Christians, Jews, Muslims, agnostics, or atheists can incorporate Buddhist practices into their lives while remaining completely true to their own beliefs.

At the core of Buddha's teachings is that we must "wake up" from our sleepwalking lives if we ever want to realize our true Self, and be able to see the true Self in others. The term "Buddha" actually means "one who is awake."

"Waking up to your own life may be easy and it may be difficult," Alison tells her clients. "It may happen in one glorious instant of enlightenment, or it may unfold over a lifetime. Life can be like devouring a fully ripe mango — juicy, fresh, luscious, and sometimes a little messy. Are you ready to begin?"

33

ARE YOU CREATING YOUR LIFE?

My session with my coach today focused on his own life's evolution from the many pains of a painful childhood to the discoveries, inside a seminar called The Forum (an extension of Werner Erhard's earlier work), that there were people living and teaching what he himself had learned to do on his own.

To put it simply, my coach had discovered the power of keeping his word. You can call it integrity and you can call it commitment, but it's having your whole life be as clean and clear as any single promise kept.

If my word is that I will meet you at nine, then my appearing at your house at nine has my word and my action be the same thing. So I am now creating my life by what I speak. My language is generative, not merely descriptive. And this is the ultimate in creativity, and this is what my coach coaches me in.

I think I discovered maybe twenty years ago the difference between creativity in the narrow field of art and music and creativity in one's entire life. Once I really got that, I could then see that everybody is potentially creative. So I always look for the hidden creative powers in my clients' lives when I sit down to coach them or when I pick up the phone to coach them.

Children are creative when they are born—Picasso said, "Every child is born an artist and the trick of life is to remain an artist." But most of us really don't remain artists. At least I didn't. I allowed myself to get talked out of it by worries and fears and a desire to make a living and not embarrass myself in the world of grown-ups.

That was my driving force—fear of embarrassment. If I was flying on a plane and a burst of turbulence had the plane drop, I didn't fear a crash as much as I feared what the people on the plane would think if I was a coward during the plunge to the ground.

So there isn't really a lot of room for creativity if that's your life. If you are just trying to survive embarrassment, or not have various people mad at you. Your life and mine soon become lives of avoidance and aversion. If the goal of life is to not have your spouse mad at you, you do things that please her and make you hate yourself. It ends up being a humiliating life.

And we don't have to live that way. What I discovered, through the value of having my own coach and putting myself through various seminars and workshops that put me back on track to having a good life, was that our lives can be the subject matter of creativity. We can each make our own life a masterpiece. Like coach John Wooden would say: make each day your masterpiece.

Instead of having some little narrow field of creativity in my life—like I might do a little watercolor here, or build a birdhouse there, or write a song every other year—have the entire life be a written song.

We can allow ourselves to apply the creativity that all children have—intuitively, innately—and open it back up and have our financial life creatively invented (constructed) and have our physical life be that way too.

Creativity with physical exercise, creativity with finance, creativity even with how you raise children! It's all possible. You can even be creative with how you create relationships in life versus the opposite of that—a life of fear. Without *creating* my relationships I'm just afraid I won't have enough love and approval. So I'll be making all my moves based on my own fears instead of what I want to create.

I can wake up in the morning and ask myself (given the day I have ahead), **What do I want to create with this day?** Because my day is pure opportunity.

Or I can do what's most common and that is wake up and ask myself, What do I fear? What do I dread? What do I hope doesn't happen? What can I avoid? What steps can I take to avoid what I dread the most?

And sadly that's how most people live—a full day of avoidance, trying to get around things, trying to avoid something happening—"I hope this audit doesn't happen, I hope she doesn't find out that I'm doing this, and I hope my daughter doesn't think that if I don't send her this money"—and everything is hoping that something doesn't happen; because we are using our creative imagination in the most negative, perverse way because we are using it to worry about the imaginary negative future.

The antidote to that—in my experience and in the experience of my clients— is to reconnect human beings to their innate, natural birthright of pure creativity.

If you look at kids, they are running around making up names and making up games all day. They have no identity system to maintain. Therefore they are very creative.

But then you look at adults and they just sit there.

Does anyone on the planet sit down as much as an adult? Was this body designed for sitting? And you look in their eyes. And their eyes are kind of bloodshot and nervous and darting around—"Who is a threat to me? Who might embarrass me? Who will unmask me and make me look like a fraud?"

Even when that bloodshot adult is "thinking positively" they are thinking, "Who do I connect to? Who do I need to impress and win the approval of?"

One of the best people on the planet that I know of on the subject of creativity is my friend Peleg Top. He coaches people in the world of design, and he also coaches them on how to bring the creativity of their art into their whole lives.

He teaches his clients how to create—not only projects for their clients, but how to create their own businesses in profitable ways—from their creativity, not from their fear of going out of business.

And, then, while he was in Israel recently, he literally by "accident" (I deliberately put the word accident in quotes) stumbled upon a new mentor that taught him a system for bringing out creativity through intuitive painting and drawing. So he fearlessly began to integrate that into his coaching practice and seminar work.

Peleg's life as a coach dramatizes for me the strength of intuition and pure productivity that's in all of us. (If we would just bring it back out, it would improve our whole lives.)

Whenever people are fearlessly creative in the world of business—like at Apple or Google —everyone stands up and cheers. "Oh my gosh what a great business they are! Facebook! OMG! Let's all go to the movie and watch how creative that young man was connecting everybody the way he did!!" And we cheer for it and then we go back home and don't live it. And yet it's open for anyone. Peleg says, "I remember walking into museums and looking at the art that hung on the walls and finding an incredible source of inspiration, thinking to myself, I just can't wait to start doing something like this for myself as well; but at the same time I was struggling with the resistance that would come up and that voice of my inner critic that says, 'Ah, you can't do this. You are not good enough. Don't even bother. Just keep designing for your clients.'

"Stumbling on intuitive painting and the whole intuitive art world called me and helped me connect to that part of myself that always had been hidden there and that was waiting to emerge and which I believe is in every single human being. Now that doesn't necessarily mean that painting is the outlet for everybody; but that basic human instinct to create is there. It is there for all of us."

Peleg got me thinking and remembering. I remember growing up and being in classrooms and it was time to paint or time to draw and we would look around at other classmates and notice that there were one or two maybe out of twenty-five kids who could really draw well; and then the rest of us compared ourselves to them and we began to think "I'm not good. I don't draw as well as Monica does and so therefore I'm not good at drawing" and I remember getting these ideas in my mind when I was young—I can't draw, I can't paint, I'm not good at this, I'm not good at that. Peleg says, "It's a belief. And I think you're right. It starts when we are children. It starts at that age; the same experience that you had. That self-critic is what we starting hearing as children in those classrooms—sometimes we even had teachers that said, "Peleg, only draw inside the lines." We grew up with a sense of what art is supposed to look like and never really had the encouragement to create. If you look at all the artists that are well known to us today—from Kandinsky to Picasso—the thing that made them most unique was their willingness to break the rules. They expressed themselves in a way that nobody else did. Sometimes creativity and bringing that instinct out to the world shocks people. And that's a good thing; but most of us are afraid to do that because, most of the time, we're in people-pleasing mode and we only want to create for the sake of getting good feedback from somebody. Look how good I am! Look how good my painting is! And only if you tell me 'Yes, this is good!' Only then will I feel good about myself."

Peleg takes painting into life itself. He coaches people on how to make their entire lives like that painting they are afraid to cut loose and get wild with.

His coaching confronts the inner life critic.

The inner voice of criticism is unforgettable because it was so piercing and hurtful when we first heard criticism when we were young. It's unforgettable (also unforgivable if you really look at it closely).

I notice in my own coaching clients that people actually respect and obey that voice! It's as if it were *the voice of reason* or their own conscience speaking instead of the ghost of a hurtful past.

I asked Peleg Top what he does when he coaches people like this. How does he get them to see that they are not applying their creativity to their lives?

"Creativity takes courage," he says. "A lot of people are afraid to take risks. Creativity involves a risk. So a lot of the work I do is to help clients get to the place where they are not afraid to take risks with their business because there's really no reward without risk."

I love the word "encourage." The kind of coaching Peleg is talking about "encourages" clients. There's courage in the world encourage. And it takes a lot of courage to do something that doesn't look like what the whole rest of the world is doing right now, which is what creativity is.

Colin Wilson wrote a great book called *The Strength to Dream,* and I was startled by the title—the "strength" to dream? I had previously associated dreaming with being passive and lazy... an irresponsible, weak, flighty use of the brain. When I read *The Strength to Dream,* even just seeing that title allowed me to see the other side of it. It does take strength and it does take creativity to actively dream. It was no accident that many years later Wilson called his autobiography, *Dreaming to Some Purpose.*

There was a period in my coaching life when I worked almost exclusively with sales people. One of my practices to help people get over this thing called "rejection" (I put it in quotes because there is no real rejection—you either *feel* rejected or you don't with the information you have just received)... was to ask a sales person to stop every time someone says "no" and internally translate that "no" into "Can't you be more creative than that?"

When he did that, it touched off new ideas: "I might propose something new, or change my approach, or ask more questions, or customize something..." He got into that creative mode that he never would have found otherwise. The courage to create. It can be *encouraged.*

Years ago a company hired me to talk to people who had lost their jobs. They were laid off and now were facing looking for another job. Soon they understood that the more creative they were willing to get, the faster they would get a new job. I said, "Pick any company you would want to work for and you can work there if you are willing to be creative enough in how you apply." Many people didn't even want to hear that. They kept coming back to me and saying, "What am I supposed to do? When do I send a thank you note? Do I send it after the interview?" And I would say, "Listen to yourself. You are trying to find out exactly what everyone else does." If people are going to hire someone who they think is going to do a better job for them than all the other people applying, why try to be like everybody else?

I often use the approach of Jerry Garcia, who was a very creative artist with The Grateful Dead. He said the trick was not to be the best at what you do; the trick is "to be *the only one* doing what you are doing." That's a different mindset than trying to anticipate what someone wants from you. It always produces a different mindset when I ask, "How creative can I be with it?" Or, "What can I do that no one else does?"

Peleg recently visited a Pablo Picasso collection at a Seattle museum.

"It was worth the trip to Seattle to just go look at this exhibit but what I remember most was the big letters on the wall where his quote was written, 'One never knows what one is going to do. One starts a painting and then it becomes something quite different.'"

This is the Picasso effect—that element of unpredictability in all creativity. Which is why good coaches won't even want to give you the answer to your problem. They will want to keep asking you questions until you empower *yourself*. Peleg says, "I think that's a really important distinction that a lot of people don't realize when it comes to hiring a coach. Many people think 'I'll hire a coach and he'll show me what to do.' And I have to say I was in that place myself. I initially hired a person, professionally, who I thought would coach me into what to do, but he really didn't help me connect to what I had inside myself to go to the next place. So now when I have clients who ask me that question (what should I do? which by now there is a rule—you are not allowed to ask me that question any more), they don't get an answer. The answers are inside of you. I don't want people to run their business like I think it should run. They did not live my life. They did not have my path and my journey. They have their own."

Experimentation is what Peleg's. whole intuitive painting lesson is designed to encourage in people. Keep looking for different ways to do things. How can you be more creative with these so-called problems you've got?

Why don't you try opening yourself up and seeing what else you might see? What can you play around with here? Creative problem solving is a beautiful process. Most people never test it. They never find that out. Because when their problem shows up they just shut down. They get upset and pout like little kids.

"I'm really *upset* that I have a problem!"

They stage a quiet tantrum instead of going the other direction that asks, "How can I get creative about this? How can I open my mind? What else is possible? What are some funny, out-of-the-box things that I'm going to try just to play with people's minds, just to mess with people?"

I try to use every phrase in the book to open people up—especially sales people who are so terrified that they are going to "bother" somebody! They're going to make people uncomfortable by trying to sell them something.

It's sad to me. Fear is what governs so many professional lives. But business was meant for play, not fear. Numbers are indicative of a game being played.

But it's encouraging to me that the antidote to all that fear is not some kind of huge, bold, macho courage—it's really kind of aggressive playfulness. Giving yourself permission to play.

Don't listen to the imaginary voice that keeps coming up denying permission: "PERMISSION TO CREATE DENIED!"

like it's coming up on the computer screen of the mind.

One client blurted out, "Creative experimentation sounds great, but I don't want to do anything I'll regret!"

You don't have to regret anything—that's optional. Regret is absolutely optional in this world. You can go find a painful memory and regret it and attach a story to it any time you like. You can regret everything if you want. You can say that any choice was the wrong choice, and then you can wonder about what the right choice would have been. But in the world of creativity and living an honorable life, these activities don't help. They do not make a good guide to what the next experiment should be. I would drop all of that and free yourself from all that judgment of yourself and fear about making the "wrong" choice and just jump in. Trust your inner compass.

I remember years ago going to see Woody Allen in Las Vegas when he was a stand-up comic. He was a very creative, funny guy. He started his life writing for TV shows, and then he did a standup act and that wasn't quite right for him, so he started to write little short stories for the New Yorker, and then he started to write plays for Broadway. Then he started to write movie scripts, and then he started to direct and act in the movies. Were any of these the "right" decision? Not really; he just kept jumping in and things got better and better.

So I say just jump in.

Forget about making the right choice, and forget about being afraid of your intuition leading you wrong, and forget about attaching a story of regret to a time in your life when you were doing the best you could and then now looking back you are going to attach a story of regret to it—there's no value in that.

You can't be creative when you're taking things personally. If you take your parents' comments personally, or your spouse's comments personally, you can't create.

Peleg says, "It's about putting ourselves in a place of more self appreciation—not waiting for that approval—not trying to please somebody else. I'm going to increase the way that I love myself and respect myself and put myself and my life in a constant state of self- love and appreciation. I know that's going to help me make my dreams come true."

Peleg's words are not to be confused with narcissistic self-reference. He's describing a more effective way to live. He's describing what he does to help his coaching clients turn their dreams and projects into reality.

A listener to a webinar Peleg and I were co-hosting on creativity asked a very colorful question: "How do you deal with getting swatted down with your creative idea and you just feel like a snowman who has melted into a puddle and can't get up."

Here's what I said to the melted snowman: "Great ideas are going to confuse other people. But I don't need other people's approval to move forward; I just move forward. Or if I do need their approval (if I'm in a company and I have a great idea and somebody doesn't agree, they are confused about it or can't see the value in it), then I make my choices based on what's going to keep my mood elevated so I can continue to have a creative life. But I don't want my happiness to be dependent upon what other people think of my ideas. I don't want to have it set up that way."

DO NOT FEAR FAILURE

*Failure is the foundation of success
and the means by which it is achieved.*

~ Lao-tzu

Most people want to succeed by succeeding, which makes sense. But when failure happens, it can be the best teacher ever. We realize that we're free to experiment more. And as Dale Dauten says in his classic little business book, "Experiments never fail."

"Don't be too timid and squeamish about your actions," said Ralph Waldo Emerson. "All life is an experiment. The more experiments you make the better."

One of the most common complaints of the people I coach today is this: "The people that I supervise just hate to make changes though they are constantly being required to in our highly competitive business environment. I just tear out my hair sometimes trying to get the needed changes accomplished!"

The way I respond is, "Yes, it may feel difficult to encourage people to change, but try this possibility: People may prefer not to change, but people love to experiment."

It's precisely because coaching is not therapy and doesn't have to follow any mental health standards that methods can be unorthodox, creative, provocative, and unforgettable.

Michael Neill was coaching a friend of mine by phone when my friend confessed that he had been procrastinating, out of fear and anxiety, about writing a short article for a well-known business magazine. Michael said, "Really? Are you near your computer?"

My friend said, "Yes, it's right here."

"Good. I want you to put the phone down — don't hang it up; just place it down by the keyboard so I can hear you typing — and I want you to write the piece right now, the entire piece, start to finish, and when you are complete pick up the phone and tell me."

My friend was startled by the request, but he did it. He wrote the piece and thirty minutes later picked up the phone and said, "Are you there?"

Michael said that indeed he was.

And my friend had written a rather brilliant article.

That's not a technique; it's an impulse based on a commitment to have your client's life get better with each coaching session, whatever that takes at the moment. It's a continuous call to action versus a call to plumbing the depths of one's emotions as psychologists do.

And this is not to demean or diminish the role of psychotherapy. It has its important place. In fact, some people who think they need coaching are better suited for psychotherapy. Psychotherapy is about healing the past. Coaching is about creating the future.

I have a friend who is a wonderful, compassionate coach. But she has a strict "no crazies" rule for her practice. (Notice how politically incorrect phrases are the best. They are so functional in a world gone mad with enforced sentimentality.)

I was politically incorrect when I ran a blog entitled, "You Had Me at RETARDED." But when people read the whole piece and linked to the wonderful Christopher Dorris video of the same name it made perfect sense.

Can you get coaching from a movie or the internet? I believe so. I receive a lot of inspiration from the internet blogs and email messages of Matt Furey who coaches people in fitness and internet business expertise.

In a recent message Matt recalls watching a clip from the movie *Miracle* – the movie about the USA's improbable (impossible?) Olympic ice hockey victory over the Russians in 1980. A victory of amateurs over professionals. Matt enjoyed the clip so much that he purchased the DVD and had it sent to him by overnight mail. Then he watched the movie with his son and watched it again the next day.

In the movie there is one moment when coach Herb Brooks has his team repeat their conditioning sprints over and over, shouting, "The legs feed the wolf!" Matt stopped the movie and wrote that down. The legs feed the wolf! It was a powerful, poetic expression of something Matt had been taught by his own great coaches over the years, Dan Gable and Karl Gotch: conditioning is the ultimate move. If you're wondering what a good move to learn would be—in hockey, in wrestling (Matt's sport) or anything in life—conditioning is it. The well-conditioned legs feed the wolf.

In the very same morning I read Matt's inspirational piece, I couldn't wait to go out and do some sprints myself.

35

BECOMING VIOLENTLY ORIGINAL

Be regular and ordinary in your life, like a bourgeois,
so that you may be violent and original in your work.

~ Flaubert

When I coach people who are stuck and not doing things they wish they were doing I often see that they are over-identified with their personal traits and qualities.

They have been hypnotized by the appearance of consistency in their habits and have started to believe in the permanence of their characteristics. This habit can be absolutely spellbinding, like watching Alfred Hitchcock's *Psycho*.

So my work as a coach is to break the spell. To hear that screeching music that comes up while a person is telling me what they are like and always do given their permanent characteristics.

A client talked to me recently about how trapped he felt in the limbo he was in between his old life habits of boredom and disappointment and the new exciting person he wanted to be.

He so wanted to change his life and live his full potential that he could almost taste it. Why was he stuck? Why couldn't he develop the willingness to live differently? What were all these frustrating feelings about and where were they coming from?

Because I'm a coach and not a compassionate therapist I didn't care. I didn't need to empathize or have a long drawn-out examination of the origins of his feelings.

So I told him his pyramid was upside down.

Remember those food pyramids we used to have on the wall in grade school classrooms? It turns out they were all wrong! Hello, obesity epidemic!

My client had his own pyramid wrong, too, because he had thoughts and feelings at the very top. Those were the things he thought he needed to study and figure out and understand before he could transform himself into a man of pure, adventurous action.

He should have had action on top and thoughts and feelings on the very bottom. You become a man of adventure by taking action, not by figuring out why you don't feel like doing it yet.

Once you are able to see that beliefs, thoughts, and the feelings they produce are just inconsequential clouds passing in the sky, you are free.

Or like that transcendent coach Byron Katie says, when the beliefs are seen to be the nebulous hallucinations that they are, "That leaves a lot of energy freed up to make amazing changes in the moment, because it's so clear, none of the options are hidden. It's a fearless state of being. The mind notices that the kind way is the brilliant way. There's no limit to it."

36

HOW TO KNOW YOUR TILT SWITCH

Pinball is a type of arcade game, usually coin-operated, where a player attempts to score points by manipulating one or more metal balls on a playfield inside a glass-covered case called a pinball machine.

~ Wikipedia

No matter what technology I write about, it will be outdated by the time this book is in your hands (or on your iPad... or whatever has replaced the iPad as the next coolest thing).

So I am okay with being outdated. In fact I don't even mind going way, way back.

Do you remember pinball machines? Do you remember the rock opera *Tommy* by The Who about a pinball wizard? Remember that "deaf, dumb and blind kid" who sure played a mean pinball?

My own life coach and I go back as far as pinball. We have been working with each other for over fifteen years. He often coaches me with vivid parables and metaphors. He illustrates what I can't yet see with a fresh, dramatic example that allows me to finally *see*. He doesn't want me to simply understand it or get it. He doesn't even want me to "grok" it. He wants me to actually see it. That's why he creates these vivid visuals (he calls them distinctions) for me to go home with and never forget.

So one day he asked me to picture a pinball machine. Not too hard for me to do given my wasted days and wasted nights spent in many a bar in my early life.

He asked me if I remembered people trying to shake the game and bang the side of the case to help guide the ball to hit more markers and ring up more points, and if you tipped the board too much the sign would say "TILT!" and that game would be over and you'd lose points that way. So trick was to learn just how much you could move and bang the board around without getting a TILT.

Yes, I remembered all that.

"Do you know how the game knows you've gone to far?" Steve Hardison asked me.

"Not really."

"There's a tilt switch in the game. Built in. And it looks like this."

At which time Hardison made a circle with his fingers on one hand and then put one finger inside the circle to illustrate the switch.

"When the switch moves too far over, it hits the inner edge of the circle and registers TILT," he said. Then he showed me with his hands.

"I see," I said.

"So what you now want in your life is to widen that circle. To keep widening that circle so that when the tilt switch tips it still doesn't register TILT and you can keep playing and keep scoring points."

"How do I widen the circle?" I said.

"By doing things you are not used to doing. Challenging yourself. Going a little too far. Going beyond what is comfortable. Each time you do that the circle widens."

And he made the circle with his hands again, and then made it wider and wider, and then he put his finger in it and made me see that the finger could tip and move over and still not hit the edge of the circle.

Hardison was trying to show me that there wasn't anything special about himself. Even though people were always telling him how bold he was and how amazing he was in his ability to approach anyone and ask him or her anything, he said, "You can do that, too. I wasn't that way always. I started with…. (and then he showed me a very small circle around the tilt switch of his finger)… this circle… and I just did it and did it and it got wider and wider. Anyone can do what I do. Anyone."

From that day on I couldn't get the tilt switch out of my mind. It was an indelible visual metaphor for being bold and challenging myself to always go a little further. To push the envelope. To step up. To stretch myself whenever I could.

Of course my coach would make sure I didn't forget to do this. One time I sent him a training proposal I had written to a company who wanted me to train their sales people. I called Steve to ask him what he thought of the proposal.

"It was great," he said. "Although I caught a typo."

"Oh really? Where is it? I'll fix it. I want it to look clean and professional."

"The fee you proposed was missing a zero at the end."

He'd wanted my $8,000 fee to be $80,000 dollars. You can begin to see now, maybe, why his huge fee is something I always earn back rather quickly from being coached by him.

37

READY TO GET PHYSICAL?

Great ideas originate in the muscles.

~ Thomas Edison

In *The 4-Hour Body*, a book that coaches you hard on losing fat and gaining strength, Timothy Ferriss recounts a time when he was on an island with billionaire entrepreneur Richard Branson.

Twenty people sat around listening to Branson's wisdom about innovation and wealth. Someone asked the final question, the question most everyone wanted the answer to, "How do you become more productive?"

Branson sat a moment... and then spoke his answer: "Work out."

What? I thought we were talking about the mind? The brain! Strategy! Innovation! What do you mean, *Work out*?

It has taken me years to see the wisdom in what Branson said. And it came... not from believing it... but rather from testing it. Trying it.

A good coach isn't afraid to move your body. He won't just fix his mind on your mind.

Stephen McGhee is one of my favorite coaches of all time. Every time I refer people to him for coaching, I get nothing but the best feedback on what it has done for their lives. Stephen is a life coach with a specialty in re-introducing his clients to their bodies.

He goes out into the world with people and puts their bodies into the whole mind/body/spirit equation. And I've found over the years in my own life and in the lives of clients I've coached, that when the body gets left out of that equation, it's not a good outcome. You can't get an optimal result. Body-neglect brings the other two things (mind and spirit) way down.

But when you lead with the body, the other two always follow. Of the three elements, mind, body, and spirit, the *body* is the only one that can get the other two to automatically rise up with it!

If you can get up and walk and move your body, the mind and the spirit will follow!

Most people try to do it the other way around.

They wait until they *feel like* moving the body. They think they've got to get their mind right before they exercise. Or they have to be in the right kind of mood or spirit and *then* they will dance, or *then* they will swim, or *then* they'll run or lift weights or play basketball. And that's why people are so out of shape. That's exactly why — because their bodies wait for inspiration instead of just diving in.

Everybody talks about the mind-body connection. I hear people say, "I'm a coach of mind/body/spirit" — but they've got it in the wrong order — they are misleading everybody — at least in my experience.

If you were to lead with the body, amazing things would happen. And you don't have to wait to be in a particular mood. You don't have to figure out if your psychology is precisely right or if the stars are aligning or if your DNA is perfect — you don't have to wait for anything. The action itself is what lifts you to act.

Stephen McGhee is in great shape. He climbs mountains, he runs, and he does yoga.

"Once I begin to really move my body," says McGhee, "there is an enlightening element that occurs in my entire life. It's like the body starts moving, the heart starts pounding, the blood flows, and the thinking gets clearer. So the progression is body, mind, and then spirit. So suddenly then there is this enlivened spirit that comes from moving my body."

As a life and leadership coach McGhee noticed that there were a number of his clients he could see were struggling with their bodies.

"They were overweight," he says, "and yet they were wanting to create something magnificent in the world, in their business, in their life, but they were being stopped by their body. They couldn't see it."

Seeing this gave McGhee an idea. He wanted to do something big so he decided to bring a group of men with him on a nine-month coaching program. He decided to start with the physical and then flow into the emotional, mental, and spiritual ways of being that supported people in growing and getting stronger in their lives and in their businesses.

"I wanted it to culminate with a huge goal," he said. "I didn't want this to be something based in theory in a seminar room where we only talked about moving our bodies. So I created a program called The Aconcagua Man Project which culminates in our climbing a huge mountain summit after nine months of exercising together."

He took his clients through nine months of mental strengthening and emotional stability, to summit out a very big mountain in Argentina called Aconcagua, which happens to be 22,834 feet to the top.

His core message to his clients: "Put your ass on the line and get everything off the couch."

Aconcagua is the tallest mountain in the world outside of Asia. And this very sense of adventure is one thing that sets life coaching apart from business consulting and from psychotherapy.

I'm reminded of the old sports coaches' saying (and it's been attributed to so many coaches now I have no idea where it began), "It's not the will to win that's important; it's the will to prepare to win."

McGhee agrees, "That mountain is not something that you want to be unprepared for. The statistics on the mountain are about thirty percent of all people that attempt the summit actually make it and, of course, our intention as a team is that we all make the summit."

That's the physical side of the coaching project, but there's another side, too. McGhee and his group of clients call it the inward summit.

"It's a realization that each of us physically has a place where we think can go to," McGhee says. "Then I have them go a step beyond that."

Going beyond where you think you can go is exactly what coaching is for. I realize with my own coaching that I never would have dared to do what I did with my professional life had I not had a coach.

McGhee says that the human body is an example of our holding back. "The body can do more than we think it can," he says. "And we as a society have gotten so lazy with our bodies that we want to do it in twelve minutes a day. We want turtleback abs in twelve minutes a day. It just doesn't work."

I've tried to get McGhee, who is forty-eight, to admit that he has down periods when he forgets or simply doesn't feel like exercising. I asked him to tell me about when those periods happen for him. This was his response: "It is not worth it to me to not exercise. I had one of the greatest compliments recently from a person who said, 'You are the most vital person I have ever met.' When I heard that I immediately thought, 'It has a lot to do with taking care of the body.' I mean, there's meditation, there's affirmations—there's all that stuff—but until the space is cleared through my body, I can just forget about it. Because if I don't exercise, my mood changes, the world looks different,

I'm more cynical about the world and the world situation. All I need to know is that I feel better after exercise. So it's not in my world that I would consider not exercising."

The vitality McGhee radiates is part of the reason his coaching practice is so successful. People love his energy. They love being in his presence. When he coaches business leaders, they open up to more exciting ranges of possibilities for their future.

Like so many people who have become enlightened to the power of living a committed life, McGhee can trace his inspiration back to a negative experience. This once again illustrates the value of "bad" experiences in life. It's a paradoxical factor that Napoleon Hill called "inspirational dissatisfaction." I'll often use it with new coaching clients. Let's find where you are most dissatisfied in life, and let's use that as inspiration for creating a new future.

McGhee was twelve when he contracted Osgood-Schlatter disease. It severely limited the movement of his knees. When all his friends were out playing football or baseball he couldn't. For ten months he had to stay sitting at home while the world outside played.

McGhee remembers that painful period: "When that finally healed up, I can remember making a decision — a choice — that I would *always exercise*, because I got to feel what it was like not to."

Some of the men who joined him for the mountain climbing project were out of shape. McGhee brought in a professional trainer to work with them, and said, "But it really started, and this is important for everybody who is out of shape, with the important foundation-setting time. So anyone thinking, 'It's time for me to start to move my body again,' it's important to start slowly. So we took two months of building foundation for these guys that were not in particularly great shape. So we weren't carrying heavy packs; we weren't running up mountains. We were doing core abdominal work at the beginning. And think about it. A lot of our strength comes from our core and our legs. People think it's big biceps — like Popeye. Remember Popeye? He ate a lot of spinach and he had big arms, but I don't know how strong his core was. The core is your abdominal area, so that's strengthening it through sit-ups; or there are other ways to do it, but that is very important when one begins a physical regime, because everything comes from there. You have a lot better chance of staying healthy without low-back problems or any other complications from heavy exercise."

McGhee's group took two months to build the core. All the while he was also coaching them in the core stability of their business and financial world, as well as family relations.

There's a core there too.

There's a principled, committed life versus a life of pleasure, pain and ego — the life of seeking love and approval from others. A life lived in vain. Coaching addresses the whole life of the client. Not just his abdominal muscles.

After the two months of core work, McGhee's guys knew that in six months they would be climbing Aconcagua — one of the toughest mountains in the world.

"It really shows how quickly and how powerfully a person can get in top condition," said McGhee.

During the training McGhee saw that there was an even greater connection between the body and the spirit than he had previously appreciated. (Coaches often become inspired by their clients.) He saw his clients grow strong.

"When one starts to get his or her body in shape, all kinds of possibilities start to emerge," he said. "No longer is a person distracted by twenty pounds of overweight excess fat. Suddenly they are moving their body better, so they are thinking more clearly, and all of a sudden they are saying, 'Let's talk about my having an extraordinary relationship with my wife.'"

38

HOW TO BE ALIVE TO LIFE

Self concept is destiny.

~ Nathaniel Branden

Dr. Nathaniel Branden always says that self-esteem is the greatest predictor of success in life. And self-esteem begins at the physical level. Whether you feel vibrant or in shape affects your whole self-concept. Even in a business meeting.

In his book *100 Ways to Improve Your Writing*, Gary Provost writes about best-selling author James Michener and how he would "actually go into training like a boxer before he began a book, so the least you can do is take a few deep breaths, put your pulse rate into second gear, and deliver a supply of oxygen to the brain."

We all get glued to the TV during the Olympics, and we are so excited that health club memberships go up during those weeks. It would be great if we could just have that be a daily thing for us too. To have our lives lived inside our own Olympic Village of the mind.

Or we could just sit around and get more depressed.

Dr. John Ratey is an MD who has devoted his life's research to studying the effect of exercise on the brain. His book *Spark* is highly recommended. Many of the psychiatrists he meets with have no clue about exercise and how it relates to depression. They just want to work with the pharmaceutical companies to come up with more and more prescriptions. And many of those drugs list "suicide" as a possible side effect of taking the drug. Suicide would also certainly eliminate the depression, but there has to be a better way.

Dr. Ratey says that most psychiatrists just don't know this:

> Toxic levels of stress erode the connections between the billions of nerve cells in the brain or that chronic depression shrinks certain areas of the brain. And they don't know that, conversely, exercise unleashes a cascade of neurochemicals and growth factors that can reverse this process, physically bolstering the brain's infrastructure.

Stephen McGhee gets calls from his team during the business week thanking him for the difficult training they did over the weekend on snowy mountains in Colorado. They tell him they feel more *alive* than they ever have before. McGhee reflects on how glad he is, as a coach, to be so focused on the physical, and to have being alive and vibrant the central characteristic of his own being.

"People want to hire coaches who are alive to life," he says.

That reminded me of something. Michael Neill was doing his Super Coach Academy in New York and invited some people over from a coaching association to sample it and sit in and see what he was delivering. When they found out that he was charging $10,000 per coach to attend, they became infuriated and refused to have anything to do with him. They pointed out that most of the "coaches" (notice I use quotes there) in their associations were making less than $20,000 a year as coaches, and they thought it was criminal that he was charging so much.

No wonder, with that victim mentality at the top, that those so-called "coaches" were making so little. And it was also funny. How can you sell yourself as a success coach when you yourself are not successful? What do they say to prospective clients? "Hire me! I'll help you get anything you want…I'll help you dream big and reach that dream… please hire me. Which Starbucks do you want to meet me at? It has to be a Starbucks because I have no office. And it has to be in my bus line because I have no car. But I can help you reach any goal you set."

So I think maybe it was an association of homeless coaches — that's what I said to Michael. Maybe it wasn't an association of professional coaches. Maybe he got it wrong. He could have had them all over to the Academy and formed a soup line for them.

McGhee is right. If a coach cannot first take care of himself and succeed and be vibrant and strong, imagine now going to someone and saying "What do you want to achieve? You name it and I'll help you get there!" And then you look at the guy and he's out of shape and out of money. This is one of the most hilarious parts of our profession. There are many amusing things about the work we do and this is just one of them.

The coaching profession has gotten so hot and popular that everyone now wants… not only to *have* a coach… but to be one. I had a cab driver in L.A. tell me he was a coach on the side and he gave me his card. I gave him a book of mine as I left the cab and he said, "Oh I know who you are! I've read this book!" Someday he and I will coach each other.

Most people think, "If I were to take up exercise, I would have to give up something else. The other parts of my life would get worse and they would suffer and they would go downhill." Business people especially tell me that. "If I took the time to get into shape, then I wouldn't be able to call Tokyo in the morning and do my deals!"

And this fear reveals a key element of physical training. Even more important than the training itself: commitment. Keeping one's commitment to it is even more strengthening than the workout itself.

McGhee says, "There have been days, thousands of them, where I did not feel like doing a damn thing in terms of exercise. So I might go down to the gym for twenty-five minutes, because my integrity is at stake, because I've promised myself I am going to do daily exercise. I mean, you and I have both worked with Steve Hardison, so I mean, Hello, the guy has cleaned my clock on this in a positive way so many times about doing what I say I am going to do. I honor the fortification of that in my life and the velocity of my word."

So McGhee uses exercise regimens for his clients, not just to get their bodies in shape, but to achieve one of the most powerful potentials that life coaching offers: the fortification of one's word.

He says, "We become more powerful with ourselves by just simply doing what we say, even if it's twenty minutes a day of stretching. So I'm not saying to everybody 'Go climb the highest peak in South America.' I'm saying, 'get out of bed, drink some water and some juice, throw a protein shake down, and do something that takes care of that temple of yours called your body,' because without it nothing else happens."

Years ago McGhee was a deeply stressed-out banker who got a blood clot that nearly cost him his life. He recalls, "I was doing a job that I did not like. I was still living in a world of 'have to' (you know, 'I have to do this work, I have to pay my mortgage') and I was being a total victim. The internal stress that I experienced by not being who I am had me create a problem in my body; and it was a blood clot and it got very serious and I, of course, ignored it like a lot of people do when they have health issues—we think they are just going to go away and oftentimes they don't. So I went into an emergency room on a Thursday evening, and the nurse looked at my arm and her eyes got big like a fish bowl (like this is really not good), and I ended up being in intensive care for almost eight days while they cleared the blood clot. I had a very severe reaction to the medication, which had me going into (what I refer to as) my near death experience because I literally left my body; my heart stopped for a minute and sixteen seconds according to the medical people on staff. When I finally came back into my body… and then later coming out of the hospital… I was thinking about how important keeping my body in shape was to fulfilling my purpose in life. I just can't fulfill my purpose if my body doesn't work!"

And his revelation after leaving his body wasn't just to stay in shape from now on, but it was also to shift his focus to what he could do as a leader of leaders and a life coach to individuals who were having their own slower, but just as real near-death lives.

"I went into coaching because I wanted to be someone who was making a bigger difference than I was making in the past. I could have looked at the challenge in my life—especially my medical challenge in 1990—and I could say, 'that was just unfair and wrong… that wasn't right… why me?' But what I did instead was I said 'I'm just so lucky to be alive. What a blessing! What do I want to do with this blessing?' Well, I quit the bank. That was the first step and I said, 'If not now, then when?' So that medical catalyst was a great catalyst for me. I was slower than most people. I needed a cosmic two-by-four to smack me in the head and say 'Wake up, Dude; it's time to go live your life,' and that's what I did."

To McGhee coaching and exercise are both about developing the power to make and keep commitments, which becomes core integrity.

A lot of people think "integrity" means not lying as much as you used to, or agreeing to now put most of your income on your IRS form. But integrity, the way McGhee lives it and coaches it, has to do with keeping your promise to yourself. In other words, having an integrated life. Word and action become integrated in integrity.

A lot of people think "integrity" is most useful as a word with which to shame others. I have a guy in my life with whom I had kind of a stormy relationship, and any time he wanted something from me that he didn't think he was getting, he would drag out "integrity" and try to beat me with the word like it was a big religious book. He used that word because he thought it was a good shaming word — that you can embarrass people with it.

But coaches like McGhee see it more as truth-equals-beauty-equals-integrity-equals-keeping your promise to yourself.

What about people who haven't exercised in years? How do they start?

McGhee has leadership clients who are like that. Joking about their big appetites and sloppy appearance.

"Commitment to yourself," says McGhee, "involves accepting that small things done consistently over time can make a major impact. If I were coaching someone who hadn't exercised in years, I would say, 'Tomorrow morning are you willing to get up early... (What time do you start your day — say 8 o'clock)... are you willing to get up at six, throw some protein down your body, drink some water and go for a twenty-five minute walk around the neighborhood? Are you willing to do that?'"

"Yes, I am willing to do that."

"Are you clear that you are not promising *me* that, but are you really clear you are promising *yourself* that?"

"Yes, I'm clear on promising myself that."

"So we are in agreement that you are promising yourself that you are going to get up tomorrow morning and do that. Is that accurate?"

"Yes, that's accurate."

McGhee knows they are committed now to do that themselves.

"Then I would call that person by noon that day and I would say, 'Sarah, did you get up in the morning, drink some protein, drink some water, and go walk round the neighborhood?'

"Yes, I did."

"What had you motivated to do that?"

"I promised myself I would."

"Great. Beautiful. How did you feel?"

"Oh, my God, I feel better. My whole day's been better. It's not even noon yet and I've got more done and I'm thinking more clearly than I ever have in my whole life — or in four years."

"Beautiful, are you willing to do it tomorrow?"

"Yes."

"Would you be willing to do five minutes longer?"

"Yes."

Many people ask, "How do I motivate myself to keep doing that?"

I'll answer that question myself because McGhee already talked about how this is something he has done ever since he was a boy and he just does it. But for those who haven't just done it, this is one of the great questions of all time. How do I motivate myself? The question keeps coming up over and over in so many different formats with so many clients of mine, and it came up in my own life so often.

My clients say to me, "What do I do when my motivation fades and my desire wanes?"

I want to set aside whatever can *wane*. In other words, anything that can fade or wane — like motivation, inspiration, and feeling like it — I want to factor that out.

If it's going to be 5:30 in the morning that I walk for twenty-five minutes around the neighborhood, I want to just walk; and I don't want to wonder why I don't feel so motivated, or wonder how to keep my motivation up because that's putting the cart before the horse. **What needs to occur is the walking** — not the motivation to walk; and people in our society get this backwards.

They think that in order to do something, they need to be motivated.

They are wrong.

McGhee says we have become lazy, but it's worse than that—much worse than lazy. We have become spoiled. We now believe that to do something, we need to really like it. It needs to be on our Facebook page as one of our *favorite things to do* before we even consider doing it.

We say to our children, "Do you want to eat this? Do you want to eat that? Would you like to go to Disneyland?" We are giving children all these choices and everybody's being pampered and catered to. People walk around taking their emotional temperature all day trying to figure out what they feel like doing.

And they come to me and ask, "How do I get myself to feel like exercising?" And my answer is that's not the problem. It's the fact that you are not exercising. That's the problem. It's not that you don't feel like it. The fact that you would even ask that question is the problem because you think you have to feel like doing something before you do it.

So it would be like saying, "If my house burns down, how do I get myself to feel like running outside?"

No one would have to get themselves to feel like it. They would run outside first and then check in with their feelings later. The same is true, I found in my world, with exercise. It wasn't about getting myself to feel like doing it. It was about doing or not doing. I'm going to do it or not do it. And that's the only question.

So all the people who wrestle with and torment themselves over trying to find the motivation to do something are really missing out on a life out there that would be there for them if they would just *do* these things.

McGhee says, "It is not supposed to be easy. We want it to be easy. Why would we want exercise to be easy? The whole point is that we get to experience something that's uncomfortable. That's why we push ourselves. That's why we watch great athletes stand on a podium with the National Anthem playing in the background and we all tear up. Because we know they pushed beyond what was easy. And we are all Gold Medalists if we would just move our bodies and move our minds and our spirit in the direction of 'this is good for me' and 'sometimes what's good for me isn't easy.'"

39

LIFT YOURSELF FROM NOTHINGNESS

*Then, suddenly, I knew not how or where or when,
my brain felt the impact of another mind, and I
awoke to language, to knowledge of love, to the usual
concepts of nature, of good and evil! I was actually
lifted from nothingness to human life.*

~ Helen Keller

Anne Sullivan was Helen Keller's teacher and dare we say life coach, although the phrase was not around then.

Helen Keller was lost and confused and asleep while awake. Then she got it when language flowed in. The little girl felt such joy.

If we are to create anything, it begins in language.

Coaching has your brain feel the impact of another mind. And one of the areas my brain most needed coaching in was selling. Once the coaching had its impact, I was able to write about the true nature of selling, which is joy. "Joy" is as powerful word as you can find on our language.

So I wrote a book called *The Joy of Selling*. The title was a deliberate choice, even though it was jarring and hard to swallow to those who thought that selling was difficult.

My whole point in that title and in that book was that once I learned to really *enjoy* the selling process and not fight it, I got successful. Once I stopped being confused about whether somebody saying "no" meant rejection, then selling actually became a thrill for me. It became something that I got good at and it was fun to do. It took many years to see the light. But once I saw the light, it happened almost overnight. Thanks Coach.

I was struggling with it for a long time. I had deep negative thoughts about it, and it took me a long time to unravel those and take a fresh approach and start over again and start selling with the idea of fun being the main objective. Money and fun. Who knew that the two went together? I had thought it was the opposite. Money and pain. That was my old belief system.

I remember so well the line from the Warren Beatty, Julie Christie movie *McCabe and Mrs. Miller.* There's a poignant moment in the movie when Beatty as McCabe says, "All you've cost me so far is money and pain…."

I saw that movie many times in my youth and would often repeat that line from the movie with my friend Fred. We'd mention an ex-girlfriend and we would both imitate Beatty's voice saying, "Money and pain."

So it meant a lot to me to see (the light!) that there could be such a thing as *joy* in selling.

After I really got the hang of selling myself, I started training sales people and sales teams and they began to have successes, too. Moving over from pain (victim) to joy (owner). I was in over twenty Fortune 500 companies at the level of sales staff and leadership teams doing my owner-victim sales training. Because there is a way to train this and to work with people and teach them how to enjoy it; and the more enjoyment people created for themselves, the more successful they were at selling. It wasn't the other way around.

Most people think it happens the other way around: Once I start selling I'll enjoy life more.

A lot of times when I would get into a group or a company, the book would get passed out to them; and they would look at the title *The Joy of Selling* and just laugh bitterly. "Oh, my gosh, it's the most dreadful profession in the world. It's the hardest thing to do. And he thinks it's some frivolous thing like the joy of cooking?"

And I noticed, too, when I started coaching coaches and putting them in my coaching school, that the part of coaching that they had the biggest struggle with was *how to sell coaching*.

It really isn't a big mystery as to why selling and sales is difficult for so many people. It's in the culture, it's in the movies, it's in the novels, it's on TV, it's in the media, and it's even in our educational system. The demonization of the profit motive is everywhere!

I noticed when my children were going to school, there was never an hour—not even one hour in the hundreds of thousands of educational hours—spent talking about commerce, or about the global marketplace and how to sell something and enjoy doing it. Selling was the necessary evil that greedy profiteers knew how to do. Good people don't do that kind of thing. Good people spend their time taking care of others.

Selling was always referred to as being greed-based, or as something you had to do as a last resort. Soon in our minds we *knew* that the most difficult part of all of life would be to sell somebody something!

No wonder it's hard to learn. Look how we've been programmed.

Well. It gives a lot of business to coaches who can teach clients to get good at selling. Coaches who specialize in that— like Brandon Craig, but I'll get to him in a minute.

Back to my sociological analysis: Movies would come out like *Wall Street* wherein the villains would always be anybody who had a company or who was involved in any kind of corporation. It's still true today in movies. So kids growing up in our country have no real positive way to relate to sales as a joyful activity. They don't see it as an exchange of value, where both sides can win, where the economy can move forward and people can advance their lives.

It's thought of as a *last* resort. If you can't catch on with some honorable altruistic organization, then you might have to go sell for a living as a very last ditch desperation move if you can do nothing else.

Now every once in a while someone comes along who is just a natural at selling—even though there might have been a lot of work behind the naturalness—like being a missionary, and selling things at a young age. Brandon Craig is one of those people.

I met Brandon many years ago when we both worked at a corporate training company and I was giving seminars. But I was only giving seminars because Brandon was selling the seminars. He was out in the world, a young guy, going into companies and corporations and picking up large checks. He sold my goal achievement training— and he led the team in sales! Everywhere he went to work after that, in telemarketing sales—any kind of sales—he would always rise to the top, even nationally. He was what I call a natural—like Redford in the baseball movie. He just loves it. He loves talking to people. He loves the whole concept of selling and has really strong principles and skills with sales.

Brandon agreed to come to one of my coaching schools to sit in and watch how that works and to help the other coaches in the school. He coached a number of those people in the school on how to sell their coaching services. And since that time Brandon has now become a powerful business coach. Whenever I have a client who is just totally stuck and I can't move them in the area of sales, I bring in Brandon and Brandon works with them for a while and then I get reports that they have had great breakthroughs and they are selling now like never before.

Brandon is a master. Not just at selling. He owned his own company that built beautiful wrought-iron gates, and he would sell and train his people to sell all day and has responded beautifully to the recession. He was in the construction-related industry with housing in Arizona—just the worst thing (or maybe the best thing) you could ever be in if you were going to be a victim of circumstance— and he sold through this whole thing and was successful in the face of dire warnings and worries.

Brandon sees sales as profoundly beautiful and a deeper and more pervasive practice than we realize.

"We are all salespeople in our own way and we are selling ourselves to our friends and our family," he says. "We're selling ourselves to our employer, to our employees, because we are constantly communicating. I would even introduce to you the idea that we also sell ourselves to ourselves. We have to buy into something all the time."

That would be a great thing to master. But so many people think selling is pushy. They are afraid that to try to sell something is bothersome. They'll end up being disliked. A friend wondered about how to better sell his music and dance lessons "without being pushy about it," and I put him in touch with Brandon, who told him: "Being pushy is what you might feel if you are not really communicating the value. If you have a music school that provides a valuable service to someone, and if your existing students love it and appreciate having it so much that they are willing to write a check for it on a continual basis, then that's exciting to communicate to others. You'd want to tell everybody! You'd want to take that chance... the chance to explain what occurs in the school for people. Let's not over-complicate the process. It's really a very, very simple process. Sales is about being able to communicate with your potential customer what it is that your service or product does for them in such a way that they can see it. Because if they can see it the same way you can see it, they'll buy it."

I agreed with Brandon. I thought back to fifteen years ago when I was struggling with selling my seminars to corporations. That fear of looking pushy really meant that I was focused on me and what I was going to get out of the sale. I wasn't focused on what value the other person might receive if they knew about it—if they could see it.

Therefore, today, the fears of being pushy are a signal to me that I am still just focused on *me.* I'm worried that I'm the only one who wins in this conversation. I'm believing that money is more important than anything—even more important than music, even more important than a life-changing seminar! I always want to turn that around and say *the experience* is the exciting thing here... not the money. If I stay focused on what happens for people—and if I take the focus off me—I don't feel pushy at all. I feel excited to keep talking and keep asking questions.

When Brandon coaches people on how to sell their services he emphasizes the direct approach. He recognizes truth as beauty—and truth as an effective approach to selling.

"We're so afraid to state our true intention," he says. "So we feel like we have to dance around the real thing, but to the person we are talking to it's not clear what we are up to."

Having your own intention be clear is everything. People don't like being manipulated. They don't like bait and switch, or the indirect approach. They want to know what we want and why.

"I believe in just being really direct and honest," Brandon says. "You might ask, 'What do you see?' or 'What is it that I've showed you that you have interest in?' or 'What do you not have any interest in?" or "What is it that you hesitate about? What is it that we need to spend more time together on? What do you see value in?' Those are the kinds of things that have the other person become part of the process so you always know where they are."

Coaching, at its best, always seems to improve the client's relationship with reality. Like Brandon does when he coaches people on how to sell. The more I know about what my prospect is really thinking at every moment, the better I will do when I am selling him or her something.

Dysfunction occurs when we don't want to know. When we fog things over with pleasantries and go unconscious. It's as if we can't handle the truth. But coaching shows us, almost always, that the truth we don't think we can handle will actually be what wins the trust of another person.

A final point Brandon stresses in his coaching is belief itself. Having a strong belief in your product or service when you go out to sell it. Because Emerson was right when he said, "Nothing great was ever created without enthusiasm." That's especially true of a great sales relationship. Enthusiasm, more than anything else, sells.

A guest in a seminar I was delivering on sales had an interesting question. He said, "I've never gone out into the field to sell something and it's something I'd like to try. What should I do first? Is it better to first acquire good sales skills or better to know my product deeply enough?"

I told him I would know the product, love the product, be crazy about it, be enthusiastic about it, be an encyclopedia of information about the product, be obsessed with it; *and* if I wanted to succeed at sales, I also want to get curious about how other great sales people do it. Get those books and audio programs. Even consider getting a coach like Brandon.

I had a young man call me the other day who was just starting his career in real-estate sales in California. He was a young man with a good company, and they offered a lot of ongoing training to him in how to sell real estate. Why was he calling me?

"I want to get the main part right," he said. "I read a book of yours and realized that I didn't want to wait all the years you waited to learn what you learned from Steve Hardison. I want that now. I want to master self-motivation and commitment. I don't want it to have to come from my company or my family or society. I know that all of that is fear-based."

The first commitment would be to be great at what you do. Not good, but great, and to be great for the fun of it, not to please anyone else or make an impression. If I'm going to sell and enjoy it, then I want to be really great at it. That's the big problem with seeing sales as the necessary evil of our system—as "the hard thing"—the one thing that's difficult to do. If I approach it that way, it will always be hard for me.

Brandon Craig stresses this belief factor too. "If somebody said they want to become a salesman, I would say find something you really believe in. Because we have far too many people out there representing products and services they really don't believe in. They are wasting a lot of time. It doesn't serve you and it doesn't serve the company you are working for and it certainly doesn't serve the customer. So once you find something you believe in and you understand what it is, next you've just got to be able to communicate that and communicate it at a level where you are willing to be completely honest and have integrity in every conversation."

Brandon also coaches people on the power of measurable, doable daily process goals versus huge heartbreaking soul-destroying deflationary outcome goals. Stressing the simplicity of a successful sales day, he tells his coaching clients: "Make an agreement with yourself on what you plan to do when you sell. A lot of people go backwards. They say, "I'm going to sell twenty-four units this week." But that's backwards and ineffective. Because they don't really understand how to get to the number twenty-four. They think that number, all by itself, is going to drive them. And although I recognize the value of having a goal, there's more value in making an agreement with yourself on what you are going to do about it. Right now, in this present day, so that it's actionable. So you are better off saying, "Today I'm going to make seventeen sales calls, and tomorrow I'll make seventeen sales calls," and then actually honor the agreement you have made with yourself so you can get some power in your performance."

But what if I'm reluctant to make those seventeen calls? What if I have what the sales training industry politely calls "call reluctance"? Brandon says, "Handle your fear ahead of time. Be prepared. Do that by recognizing that whoever it is that you are calling could potentially benefit from your call. But you can't do that from a position of fear."

Many sales training companies have made tons of money training sales teams to overcome call reluctance. It's a huge problem in the world of selling. I had that problem myself in very profound degrees! It wasn't until I brought in my own coach that the problem went away. And I didn't "overcome" call reluctance; I overwhelmed it. I crushed it. My coach explained that it would either have to be that, or not work with him. No middle ground.

Call reluctance! It sounds rather innocent doesn't it?

The worst part about this seemingly mild problem of call reluctance is that it becomes life reluctance, getting-out-of-bed reluctance, joining-society reluctance, being-a-part-of-civilization reluctance. It's a slippery slope.

It's an unwillingness to join the world and play in the global games.

And it is so much fun to really stare it down and look at why I am resistant—what it is about? What I am going to say when I call people? Why am I reluctant to say it?

I want to change what that is until I am excited to say it—so I can't wait to say it. Because if I don't have what I am saying be something I'm so happy to be able to offer, then none of this will work! I want to have my call be something that gives you an opportunity! I want to realize and make real to myself (as if reality were on my side) the fact that if I hadn't called you, you would have no way of knowing about this opportunity for this service.

If I don't get myself into that internal position to come from, then of course I'll have call reluctance. I'll always have it. And like Brandon Craig says, "Do I believe in it? Do I believe this call would serve the recipient of the call?" Because if I believe that, why would I resist it? I am helping you. I'm not reluctant to help you or offer you something really nice.

If I am a waiter and I'm offering you dessert or coffee after your meal, I don't have resistance to that. I walk up and offer it because you might like that. And so, it's pure service that I offer it. So why do I not see my sales call as a service to someone? I can if I make the internal adjustment.

There are two ways to fix fear. One is internal and one is external. I can fix it by doing the thing I am afraid of over and over and over enough times so that it's just easy and almost boring for me. That's one proven way. Or I can do it by cleaning myself up internally and altering my beliefs so that my belief is different when I make the call.

It's best to do both.

The external way would be — whether I'm reluctant or not — I'm going to make the seventeen calls. I'm going to put a big white sheet on my door with seventeen boxes in it; and at every call, I'm going to put an x in one box. I will not leave this office until the seventeen are made. Now there is no longer a matter of reluctance; it's just something I am doing and there can be fear or no fear or nervousness, but I am doing it anyway. If I do that again tomorrow and the next day, I'll notice the fear diminishes. That's the external way to break this thing.

The internal way is to sit with my coach and allow him to challenge my belief. He then helps me develop a stronger more useful belief, and together we keep strengthening my belief in what I am doing and dropping the negative aspect of what I believe I am doing, and the fear tends to go away that way too.

As Brandon says, "Why would someone buy anything from you if you can't muster up the courage to sell it? So you might want to get that handled before you move to the calling part."

Why would I use my blog (www.imindshift.com) to SELL my upcoming seminars and coaching schools? Why would I openly sell on a blog that people innocently read? Why would anybody ever sell anything? Why exchange value? Why not SEIZE the wealth of others and redistribute it to those with the most depressing grievances?

I got an email the other day that criticized my blogs saying, "Seth Godin would never do that. Seth expresses gratitude in his blogs. Seth never markets without permission." Seth is careful not to sell because his reputation is important to him.

My reputation is not important to me. If I can help people,

I will. I will not equate selling with harming. And that upsets a lot of people's paradigms. But if NO ONE is EVER at all UPSET with my work and communications, then I know that I am simply playing it safe and making caution my only mission.

40

I AM SEEKING YOUR DISAPPROVAL

Perhaps the most powerful coach of all time is Byron Katie. In a coaching school I was conducting, a woman raised her hand once and asked me why there were so few women in the coaching world. I begged to differ. There are as many good women as there are men.

Byron Katie says, "Personalities cannot love. They want something." I rejoice that someone has finally pointed that out. She is fearless.

Many people have subscribed to receive email messages from me. I will often try to drive people away from the membership with messages that stretch their belief systems to the breaking point. Why do I do this? Am I crazy?

No. I was doing Katie's meditative work on the belief "I need approval" and one of the turnarounds (possible beliefs that are as true or truer than the dysfunctional belief that's sabotaging my life and happiness) was "I need disapproval." And I could really see it. I need disapproval to let me know that I'm not playing things safe and that I'm out there, giving it my all—whether in a book, a talk or a coaching session.

Not disapproval for its own sake… but a willingness to push the envelope and really stretch what's expected. I will never know if I am doing that unless I get some push back.

41

RESCUE YOUR FUTURE NOW

A great coaching conversation pulls the future out of the future. Why leave your future stranded in the future? Many years ago I returned from a great Landmark Education seminar with a five-year plan for myself. I couldn't wait to take it to my coach Steve Hardison and show him. I was going to be a public speaker!

I had a five-year plan. I was proud of myself, because prior to the seminar it was just a pipe dream, and now it was a reality. It was on a piece of paper in my hands. You can't get much more real than that.

"Oh, yes you can," said Steve Hardison.

"What do you mean?" I said.

"Why do you want to wait *five years* for this?" he asked. "I've heard you speak to a room full of people."

"Oh, that was just fooling around…. don't you think it takes time? To ramp it up? Start small and build. Build a reputation over time?"

"It will take five years only because you believe it will take five years."

"Oh."

"Why not do it now?"

"Now?"

"Why not compress it and have all the things you want to do in the future take place right now?"

I got very excited. I didn't know you could do that. I didn't know you could put the future into the present moment. My five-year plan happened in five months. Five months after the plan I was getting five-figure fees for my speaking and my calendar was filling fast. So does coaching work? People always ask me, does it really work? Or is it just some kind of feel-good thing?

42

WE DON'T NEED NO EDUCATION

Coaching was created for those who never sing.

I moved into coaching reluctantly. I would give talks and the clients would ask me to stay an extra day after the talk and "coach" various individuals.

If I hadn't been coached myself by the ultimate coach, I would be totally blind to what coaching could do. Now I was just partially blind.

I knew one thing about coaching. It would be two people talking. Two people instead of one. It would break the isolation. That sense of isolation that makes a person feels trapped in his own ego. "People say we got it made," sang John Lennon. "Don't they know we're so afraid?" That song was called "Isolation."

Coaching replaces isolation with connection.

Lennon's lyrics were often bold and brutal. Especially after he left McCartney and did his primal scream therapy emerging with this musical vow that I myself vow as well, "No short-haired, yellow-bellied, son of tricky dick is gonna mother hubbard soft-soap me with just a pocketful of hope." I wake up in the morning and take that vow.

Alas for those that never sing! That's what Oliver Wendell Holmes said. "Alas for those that never sing, but die with their music still in them."

When a guy like me dies with his music still in him, it's a shock to the pathologist when he opens the body up and the music is released. All the attendants in the autopsy room back away from the body they have now dubbed "Pink Floyd."

43

WHAT IF YOU WEREN'T AFRAID?

I must not fear. Fear is the mind-killer.
Fear is the little death
that brings total obliteration.

~ Frank Herbert

Super coach Michael Neill wrote this recently: "Whatever it is you're trying to achieve, ask yourself *what you would do if you weren't afraid.* Don't worry about whether or not you actually are or aren't afraid—just notice your answers, and notice which ones you want to act on."

"As I have written elsewhere, there is a tremendous difference between feeling the fear and doing it anyway and the freedom which comes from finding that space in yourself which is beyond fear. And the more time you spend living beyond fear, the sooner the answer to 'What would I do if I wasn't afraid?' will become 'Exactly what I'm doing now.'"

Michael and I had twenty-two wonderful, courageous people sign on to the Financially Fearless Money Mastermind for six months of abundance-muscle-building and wealth-creator lessons for those who wanted to earn the money they've always wanted to earn but were afraid to.

Life usually has three acts, (1) childhood, (2) adult victimhood, and (3) transformation.

Most people never take the stage for act three.

How does one become rich? How does one not become rich? Let's start there. Because there are a hundred ways to become rich. But only one way not to. So if we took that *one way not to* away, what a start that would be.

So if we took the fear (one way not to) away, what a start that would be. And how would we finish after that? The other hundred ways would come to you.

Some people find it offensive to talk about money this openly. Especially when politicians have promised us that money will never be a problem for us. That we will all get what we are entitled to.

> *But it's not entitlement. An entitlement is what people on welfare get, and how free are they? It's not an endlessly expanding list of rights – the 'right' to education, the 'right' to food and housing. That's not freedom; that's dependency. Those aren't rights; those are the rations of slavery – hay and a barn for human cattle. There is only one basic human right, the right to do as you damn well please. And with it comes the only basic human duty, the duty to take the consequences.*

> **~ P.J. O'Rourke**

Then there's the secret law of attraction. Another way to *not work*... not use your hands or your resourcefulness or your creative desire to serve. Soon you are demeaned into *wanting things*. It's demeaning, isn't it? It's ultimately degrading to make lists of all the material things you are wanting.

Never noticing the power you already have.

You erroneously think those things will give you power. Money, cars, homes, lovers. You think that comes first, then the power.

When you had the power all along. You just weren't using it.

I would have gladly paid $100,000 to learn what our money-coaching program delivered. In fact, I did pay that, a few times over, to learn what the program delivered. I learned the hard way. I learned that of all the powerful things you can do with money, spending it is the least powerful.

People fear money and death for the same reasons — because of the same deep primitive misunderstanding.

A child will believe a superstition if enough adults verify it and confirm it. A child will even believe in Santa Claus if enough adults confirm that he is real. It's the same process with any accepted belief. Each belief changes that child's whole life. Like money makes you secure.

Until it's deleted. Until we are willing to start over. And that's where coaching comes in. It is one sure way of starting over.

GO ASK THE DOG

One day Michael Neill just totally changed my life.

I had a phobia—I only had it for about fifty years, but it was still terrible. It was around dogs and animals. Michael invited me over to his home office and worked with me all afternoon doing a powerful mix of coaching, NLP, and hypnotherapy; and afterwards it was just amazing. The healing (re-framing, re-programming) work that he did actually worked. He brought his dogs into the room with us, and I couldn't wait to pet them and rub their bellies and get to know them.

Who was I?

I've got my own dog now. Jimmy. He has changed our lives at home. He's just such an amazing addition to my life. It never would have happened if it hadn't been for my friend, the author of the great book *Supercoach,* his modestly-named book about how he coaches people.

Some people out there in the world are as popular as Michael—writing, selling books, and doing radio and TV shows—but do they change lives like he does? I doubt it. Everything he writes about and talks about on his radio show he actually *does* for people.

Does coaching really work?

Ask Jimmy.

45

CAN YOU EXCHANGE YOUR BRAIN?

I was reading an article in the *Wall Street Journal* by Sharon Begley called "How Thinking Can Change the Brain" which I found so very interesting given that coaching is all about that.

Begley talks about research done at the University of Toronto using brain imaging to measure activity in the brains of depressed adults. Half of the volunteers received the antidepressant Paxil, and the other half received twenty sessions of cognitive-behavior therapy, "learning not to catastrophize. That is, they were taught to break their habit of interpreting every little setback as a calamity, as when they conclude from a lousy date that no one will ever love them."

The depression lifted in both test groups.

Linda Ronstadt (catch Linda singing this on YouTube), the Everly Brothers, Vince Gill and so many more have sung the song:

> *I've been cheated*
> *been mistreated*
> *when will I be loved?*

It wouldn't have been as great a song had it gone this way:

> *I've been cheated*

Been mistreated
When will I learn not to catastrophize?

But I love all this research because it has helped me reveal another thing that happens when people get good coaching... they learn not to catastrophize.

Catastrophizing can become contagious. People get on the phone and catastrophize with each other. People become addicted to their own catastrophes as well as other people's. It becomes quite compelling.

The coach who sees it and calls you on it can seem heartless at first, but stay with it. Because once the story of catastrophe disappears, the story of opportunity replaces it.

46

PROCRASTINATION IS GOOD!

*Procrastination is the soul
rebelling against entrapment.*

~ Nassim Nicholas Taleb

When I didn't have a coach and I procrastinated, I would simply tell myself that I had this terrible flaw called procrastination. It was one of my many bad habits.

But a great coach won't let you get away with that.

Negative labeling that reduces self-esteem? Not allowed! With most people this labeling is automatic. And it has no relationship to the truth.

Procrastination is a beautiful form of rebellion. It's a rebellion against other people's imaginary judgment. It's a rebellion against living other people's lives for them and reaching their goals instead of yours. Even if it's a task you were going to do just for you, if it's something you think you "should" do versus what you are truly choosing to do, you will rebel. It is your soul.

The only problem occurs when you notice that all around you is unfinished business! Chaos. Broken promises.

So how to convert the rebellion against entrapment into something better than unfinished business?

Awareness. Then practice.

My to-do list is something that looks like it's telling me what to do. And it is, isn't it? Isn't my to-do list trying to tell me what to do?

In a book called *Time Warrior* I have recommended the elimination of to-do lists and the return to the joyful single act. As with all my previous books, the content came from coaching sessions that changed me.

47

LOST, STUCK AND MISERABLE

My coaching clients often know what they "should be" doing. They know their business. They know themselves. They know a lot. Many are already quite well known and successful. And my first objective is to separate that... separate what they know... from what they live. Two different categories.

~ Dusan Djukich

Todd Musselman is a coach and speaker who has created his own powerful versions of the Owner-Victim distinctions I first introduced in *Reinventing Yourself*.

Todd says, "My first victim phase is that I would rather be lost, stuck, or miserable than ask for assistance. I would rather be fired, or divorced or dead than ask for assistance."

But then he points out that when the victim reaches out and gets help, the power of owning his own spirit starts to materialize.

"Coaching is great," he says, "because it provides a powerful space for you to fully express yourself in a way that you feel 'gotten.' It's great because it provides a space in which creating what you want in your life is the only focus."

Everyone else you talk to has his or her own focus. They all want something. They may even love you, but they want something. They have an agenda.

Your coach is the only person in your life who has no agenda. Everyone else you talk to has an agenda of some sort. Your coach only wants you to succeed.

And that's the key to the effectiveness of coaching.

48

CONFIDENCE TO DO WHAT YOU LOVE

Rich Litvin is an expert in deep, inner, natural confidence. He has worked with best-selling authors, physicians, Fortune-500 consultants, and coaches to help them achieve inspirational results, create passionate relationships and build wealth doing what they love.

He recently worked with an Olympic athlete who was struggling to fund her Olympic bid by selling calendars. She had one coaching session with Rich and the next day called to say she had raised $40,000 of corporate sponsorship.

But for much of Rich's life, although people thought he seemed really confident, it never really felt like that for him.

It looked like he was successful, but inside he felt nervous and insecure and so he felt like a fraud. He was terrified that you would find this out, so he learned all the tricks he could to appear more and more confident.

But none of those tricks worked.

He ended up feeling less and less confident. So Rich has spent the last decade learning as much as he can about how to build deep *natural* confidence. He has traveled the world interviewing the world's most confident people.

Rich also coaches. Most of his clients have already achieved a great deal in life, but they have one thing in common—they all feel like they are facing an impossible goal. And they lack the confidence to achieve it.

I have co-facilitated seminars with Rich and interviewed him on one of my webinars recently. I asked him about being nervous and whether he had butterflies even before this interview.

"That's the funny thing," he said. "Every time I talk about confidence on a radio interview, the irony doesn't escape me that I get nervous as I'm getting ready for that conversation."

I love it that he calls himself out on that. A lot of people think that coaches who teach things have to be amazing perfect experts in that category. And the truth is the best coaches are people who really had to work hard—harder than most—to achieve things and to learn how to do things. It's always true in sports. You look at all the best managers and coaches and you never remember where they played the game because they didn't distinguish themselves as players at all—they had to learn the hard way—and that's why they can teach it so well.

So it's great that Rich talks about his nervousness because it allows his clients and everybody listening to my webinar to listen better. Because when it's hard for you to do, I really want to hear about it. But when it comes naturally for you I tune out, and I think, "Ok, great, lucky you; I can't identify with you."

Rich says, "I've noticed, the more authentic I'm willing to be—the more willing I am to speak up when I feel nervous or insecure—the more I relax on the inside and those fears seem to disappear anyway."

Rich works with some clients who want confidence for themselves and also want their partners to be confident. It's a common misfire I also see in my own clients: the desire to have my family members change. Or, even more common, the desire to have my spouse or partner change for the better.

It's a total distraction to want other people to change. It's misdirected energy, and it only leads to misery. A good coach like Rich won't go there with you.

"When you desire something from someone else in a

relationship (especially in an intimate relationship), that begins to be the downfall of the relationship," he says. "Whatever you want more of you need to look at how *you* can increase that in *your* life."

So a man is projecting his own insecurities on his wife, and soon he's longing for the romance of the early dating days to return. Rich said, "There is nothing more exciting for a woman in a relationship with a man, than to have a man who is in touch with his purpose in life. A man who knows what he wants in life — a man who is clear about what he is doing is a man who feels confident, grounded, and solid... and there is nothing more attractive. So for the man who wants to inspire his wife (instead of fixing her), he can just go to that place of purpose. Just tap into that."

Does he mean that women don't love needy, confused victims who come home from work and blame everyone at work for how bad they feel? That's not an aphrodisiac? Wow. Who knew?

Actually he's so right. I've never had any of the women in my seminars come up to me and say, "You know what I love about my husband? The complaining he does about people at work when he gets home. That just lights me up. I am so connected to him when he does that. It turns me on. I light candles, I put on soft music and I just can't wait for him to come home and complain about life."

I've never heard anyone say that. It's always the opposite. People are attracted to people who own their lives. People are not attracted to victims.

And I enjoy Rich Litvin's willingness to share his own stories about when he lacked confidence, or when he failed at things.

I started my career in public speaking trying to be somebody I was not. I was going to try to hide all my failures and pretend I was Tony Robbins, or pretend I was born with a Boy Scout uniform on and I just catapulted out of the womb full of energy and I was like Tony doing karate kicks and having passion… and it just wasn't me.

My own coach Steve Hardison took me aside and said, "Why don't you just be you? Why don't you share the stories of your life and where you've come from and all you've been through?"

And I said, "Well, I don't want the audience being depressed or suicidal at the end of my talk."

And he said, "No, that won't happen. They will identify with you. You'll feel the connection right away. Just be real. Just be you. Forget about trying to be somebody successful. No one will buy that."

How true.

But soon it was amazing because I just dropped all that bad act about how great and successful I was and *I just told the truth* about my kids and me and my life and alcohol addiction, bankruptcy — I mean the whole thing. Jerry Springer's show! It almost turned out to be that, but it was powerful and surprising to me because people were able to identify with my stories, and soon I started putting more of that in my books and people started buying the books at a greater rate. People started asking me to come speak.

The coach will get you to the truth. And the truth will set you free.

49

A WORLD CRUELLY DISRUPTED

Come senators, congressmen
Please heed the call
Don't stand in the doorway
Don't block up the hall

~ Bob Dylan

My friend Will Keiper coaches international corporations and the people who run them. He has special insights that allow him to immediately transform businesses in distress into businesses that can be vital and successful again.

He works with boards and CEOs to give them harsh new life after years of passivity and neglect. When he steps back from his work, he sees that a lot of our problems are generational. Will points out that his Boomer generation has "...looked ahead to retirement and grandchildren, and easing into our seventies and eighties; but on the other hand, as pointed out by Tom Friedman, we also have been ...the grasshopper generation, eating through just about everything like hungry locusts..."

"We have been voracious consumers of credit to buy homes, second homes, swimming pools, cars, planes, vacations, electronics and whatever our kids wanted or demanded. Just as we are approaching the good life of retirement, our more-or-less stable world has been irrevocably and cruelly disrupted. An aging generation has met a financial crisis that compares with or exceeds that of the Great Depression of our parents' generation. Our fellow boomers and their children and grandchildren have been loaded with a staggering amount of national debt. The debt is so large that it threatens the very financial stability of our country, and has already diminished the US role in the hierarchy of world power. As a collective generation, our future absolutely will not unfold as we had hoped."

This fact terrifies most people in Will Keiper's generation, but not Will. His specialty is confronting distress and converting it into creative, vibrant health.

He enjoys waking people up.

He recommends that older people take another look at their lives; and instead of asking when they can retire, ask, instead, "How can I get busy and contribute?""Ongoing productive contributions must now replace golf and bridge," says Will. "We cannot live in the segregated retirement community 'reservations' where older people have in the past gone to bide their time and wait for what's next. We must rapidly access and gear up the personal power and energy that is normally downshifted about now. This is the new normal."

I've been urging Will to write a book about this for a long time. To take his powerful coaching and consulting that turns companies around so quickly, and apply it to our whole nation. Turn us around too! With more of your wisdom: "Although we have been severely impacted by events beyond our control, we can choose to make the days ahead the most vibrant and powerful period of our lives. We can turn legitimate fear of this new unknown into an unprecedented recommitment to American innovation, entrepreneurship, and job creation. We can leverage the experience, education, and wisdom we have at our disposal as a consequence of living longer and better than any prior generation. A pragmatic wartime remark by

Winston Churchill sums up what now must become our generational mantra: 'It is no use saying, "We are doing our best." You have got to succeed in doing what is necessary.' The good news is that there is a ready answer for 'Now what do I do?' It is already in you."

A few more coaches like Will Keiper in the world, and we will be fine.

50

A COACH SHOULD HAVE A COACH?

My friend and coaching school colleague, Ron Wilder, is an amazing coach and an amazing person. A high-level martial artist and classical pianist, Ron lives life to the fullest. His coaching specialty is working with CEOs to re-align their businesses so that they run at the highest productivity possible.

Ron also coaches business consultants and other coaches.

"Every coach should have a coach," he says. "Having a coach makes you a better coach because you are experiencing the very process of growth and development that you are asking your clients to engage in."

Wilder notes that being coached takes huge courage, which is one of the reasons why it is so effective at changing lives. Where else in life do we regularly schedule acts of courage?

"No wonder I'm so tired after my coaching sessions," Wilder said. "When I am being coached, I really work. Now as the coach, I'm going to ask my clients to do the same thing. In order for them to advance towards their success, they will voluntarily submit to the coaching process. If they do it fully, going all-in, they get the biggest benefit. Yet this is risky. And it is exactly what I want my clients to do. Take the risk and grow."

51

WHY NOT JUST DO THINGS?

Because most people never define the necessary required actions to get a result, they will always simply do whatever actions are comfortable at the time. They are always going with the feeling of activity instead of insisting on doing the necessary required action.

~ Dusan Djukich

People have dreams but they don't live those dreams. They talk about their dreams sometimes after a glass of wine or two, but when will the dream come true?

The first thing a good coach will do is find the dream — even if it's lodged inside a complaint about life. Then the next thing the coach will do is help transform the dream into a doable project. Vladimir Nabokov says this in *Speak Memory*:

It is certainly not then — not in dreams — but when one is wide awake, at moments of robust joy and achievement, on the highest terrace of consciousness, that mortality has a chance to peer beyond its own limits.

Pyschotherapy is all about feelings. But coaching is all about achievement... robust joy and achievement. Your coach doesn't just want you to feel better about yourself. Your coach wants you to feel what it feels like to achieve something remarkable.

The Coaches

Steve Hardison, www.theultimatecoach.net
Byron Katie, www.thework.com
Michael Neill, www.supercoach.com
Rich Litvin, www.thatconfidenceguy.com
Ron Wilder, www.alignedaction.com
Tom Rompel, www.growthstrategiesllc.com
Stephen McGhee, www.thegetrealblog.com
Brandon Craig, www.tlc5.com
Peleg Top, www.pelegtop.com
Will Keiper, www.firstglobalpartners.com
Alison Arnold, www.docaliarnold.com
Matt Furey, www.mattfurey.com
Dusan Djukich, www.straightlinecoach.com

PLEASE GO TO:
THE LIFE COACHING CONNECTION
www.tlc5.com

ABOUT THE AUTHOR

Steve Chandler is the author of dozens of books and audio programs, including the bestsellers: *Fearless, Reinventing Yourself, Shift Your Mind, Time Warrior,* and *100 Ways to Motivate Yourself.*

He is the leader of the **Steve Chandler Coaching Prosperity School** (www.stevechandler.com) and writes a popular blog called iMindShift (www.imindshift.com).

Chandler is also one of the featured coaches at TLC5.com: The Life Coaching Connection (www.tlc5.com).

Also by Steve Chandler

Time Warrior

Fearless

The Woman Who Attracted Money

Shift Your Mind: Shift the World

A Crime of Genius (coming soon)

9 Lies That Are Holding Your Business Back
(with Sam Beckford)

The Small Business Millionaire (with Sam Beckford)

Business Coaching (with Sam Beckford)

100 Ways to Create Wealth (with Sam Beckford)

100 Ways to Motivate Yourself

Ten Commitments to Your Success

Reinventing Yourself

RelationShift: Revolutionary Fundraising
(with Mike Bassoff)

The Joy of Selling

The Story of You

100 Ways to Motivate Others (with Scott Richardson)

The Hands-Off Manager (with Duane Black)

50 Ways to Create Great Relationships

Two Guys Read Moby-Dick (with Terrence Hill)

Two Guys Read the Obituaries (with Terrence Hill)

Two Guys Read Jane Austen (with Terrence Hill)

Two Guys Read the Box Scores (with Terrence Hill)

Two Guys on the Road (coming soon)

Robert D. Reed Publishers Order Form

Call in your order for fast service and quantity discounts
(541) 347- 9882

OR order on-line at **www.rdrpublishers.com** *using PayPal.*
OR order by mail:
Make a copy of this form; enclose payment information:
Robert D. Reed Publishers
1380 Face Rock Drive, Bandon, OR 97411
Fax at (541) 347-9883

Send indicated books to:

Name_____

Address_____

City _____ State _____ Zip _____

Phone _____ Fax _____ Cell _____

E-Mail_____

Payment by check ☐ or credit card ☐ *(All major credit cards are accepted.)*

Name on card _____

Card Number _____

Exp. Date _____ Last 3-Digit number on back of card_____

Qty.

The Life-Coaching Connection: How Coaching Changes Lives.................$14.95 _____

The Woman Who Attracted Money...$14.95 _____

Shift Your Mind, Shift Your World..$14.95 _____

Fearless..$12.95 _____

The Joy of Selling..$11.95 _____

100 Ways to Create Wealth (with Sam Beckford).......................$24.95 _____

Small Business Millionaire (with Sam Beckford)........................$11.95 _____

Ten Commitments to Your Success ....$11.95 _____

RelationShift: Revolutionary Fundraising (with Michael Bassoff) ....$14.95 _____

Two Guys Read Moby-Dick (with Terrence N. Hill)....................$9.95 _____

Two Guys Read the Obituaries (with Terrence N. Hill) ....$11.95 _____

Two Guys Read Jane Austen (with Terrence N. Hill)................$11.95 _____

Two Guys Read the Box Scores (with Terrence N. Hill)............$14.95 _____

Total Number of Books _____ Total Amount _____

Note: Shipping is $3.50 1st book + $1 for each additional book.   Shipping _____

THE TOTAL_____